THE NEW HEGEMONY
IN LITERARY STUDIES

Rethinking Theory

GENERAL EDITOR

Gary Saul Morson

CONSULTING EDITORS

Robert Alter
Frederick Crews
John M. Ellis
Caryl Emerson

THE NEW HEGEMONY
IN LITERARY STUDIES

Contradictions in Theory

Tony Hilfer

Northwestern University Press
Evanston, Illinois

Northwestern University Press
Evanston, Illinois 60208-4210

Printed in the United States of America

10 9 8 7 6 5 4 3 2 1

ISBN 0-8101-1952-8 (cloth)
ISBN 0-8101-1953-6 (paper)

Library of Congress Cataloging-in-Publication Data

Hilfer, Anthony Channell.
    The new hegemony in literary studies : contradictions in theory / Tony Hilfer.
      p. cm.—(Rethinking theory)
    ISBN 0-8101-1952-8 (cloth : alk. paper) — ISBN 0-8101-1953-6 (pbk. : alk. paper)
    1. Criticism—History—20th century. 2. Marxist criticism—History—20th century.
I. Title. II. Series.
PN94 .H55 2003
801'.95'0904—dc21   2002014543

For Jane
Without whom nothing

Contents

Acknowledgments

I am grateful to Bill Scheick, Jim Garrison, Dick Hocks, Mike Adams, and Bob Twombly for their encouragement and advice as I pursued this project. Also to Dave Hickey, recently certified as a genius (as if we didn't know it all along), for general intellectual stimulation. Gary Saul Morson saw the possibilities latent in the first draft of the book and what was needed to better realize them. My research led me to incisive minds I know only through their writing, some but not all of whom are represented in my works cited. I was enabled by independent-minded intellectuals running from Diderot to the many who are still holding out in our profession. I wish also to thank the readers of the manuscript drafts; my copyeditor, Rita Bernhard, whose keen eye spotted the odd—sometimes quite odd—syntactical glitch and mismatch between text and citation; and the patient and considerate Susan Betz and her excellent staff at Northwestern University Press. Finally, I owe thanks to a University of Texas faculty research grant that allowed me a semester's leave to begin developing this book. It should go without saying that any flaws or inaccuracies in this final version of my book are all my own.

Introduction

This book is about the self-privileging maneuvers of the amalgamation of post-structuralism, Marxism, feminism, and multiculturalism known as Theory. Aspects of Theory, especially feminism, have, as they say, raised consciousness but by now even these more sustainable insights have been reiterated to the point of redundancy, only rarely with any reexamination of perspectives or addition of fresh, unpredictable observations. Theory is calcifying into blindness as its discourse approaches a point of scholarly entropy where "texts" are endlessly "interrogated" by application of a set grid of predictable and unexamined assumptions. A change in the ruling ideas of literary studies generally comes about when graduate students and assistant professors see diminishing returns from them. That time may be approaching, given that some of the most creative pioneers of Theory now express repugnance at certain of its orthodoxies (Spivak; Said, "Opponents," "Politics of Knowledge"; Lentricchia).

The current influence of Theory can be explained by way of its own concept of hegemony, elaborated by the Italian communist intellectual Antonio Gramsci. Hegemony is defined by the Marxist critic Raymond Williams as a method of domination that "is seen to depend on its hold not only on the expression of the interests of a ruling class but also on its acceptance as 'normal reality' or 'commonsense' by those in practice subordinated to it" (118). It gives you "the capacity for automatic and unreflective legitimation, for being unaware of the contingency of your claims" (Terdiman, 244). Under a given hegemony "a subject or topic is so constructed as to deny further empirical observation any corrective power: the grounds for reform become the criteria of inadmissible evidence" (P. Hamilton, 1037). Some forms of power may come out of the barrel of a gun, but hegemonic power works through its control over the implicit rules of discourse: "A hegemonic order prescribes, not the specific content of ideas, but the limits within which ideas and conflicts move and are resolved" (Hall and Jefferson, 39). It is a "kind of power that generates certain kinds of questions, placed within systems that legitimate, support, and answer those questions" (Bové, 54). It works exactly in the fashion by which Stanley Fish defines an "interpretive community," that is, as a "set of tacit assumptions and beliefs within which research goes on, assumptions which rather than deriving from the observation of facts are determinative of the facts that could possibly be observed" (Fish, "Rhetoric," 211).

Hegemony is the outcome of ideology, a system of false consciousness so pervasive that it prevents itself from being critically examined. As we shall see, all versions of Theory need to assume an almost irresistible force in ideology in order to explain why Theory's "oppositional" conceptions have not been well received. As Leonard Jackson points out, "there is a strong temptation, if you think unconscious ideology is as powerful as this, when you get into power to have a go at manufacturing it. This is the route to the totalitarian society of Stalin and others. But it is a way of strong temptation for any intellectual interested in cultural theory, and impressed by the notion that most human needs are actually manufactured ones" (*Dematerialisation*, 164). English departments and academic literary journals have, to a major degree, yielded to this temptation. I draw some of my definitions from a University of Chicago Press manual that predominantly reflects the Left lexicon for literary criticism, *Critical Terms for Literary Study*. Its introduction declares that "the goal of raising consciousness about everyday culture cannot be achieved unless [the] terms of interpretation themselves are examined critically" and that "any interpretation that proceeds without examining such terms will reproduce cultural and political assumptions rather than question them" (Lentricchia and McLaughlin, ix). *The New Hegemony* accepts this invitation by interrogating what Paul Bové calls the "new orthodoxy" (64).

Theory's success in overturning the previous critical paradigms was owing to its deployment of the "hermeneutics of suspicion," a method of unmasking the unquestioned assumptions and unrecognized contradictions essential to the orderly maintenance of hegemonic discourse. Stephen Greenblatt notes the centrality of the concept of "contradictions" to both Marxism and poststructuralism: "For the former they are signs of repressed class conflicts, for the latter they disclose hidden cracks in the spurious certainties of logocentrism" (5). Leonard Jackson sees this "progressive" methodology as going back to Socrates: "the application of reductio ad absurdum arguments to our concepts" (*Dematerialisation*, 64).

Jackson notes, however, that those who apply this device to other discourses never use it to test their own. Marxism, for instance, is not argued by Marxists: "Marxism . . . is a set of fundamental assumptions rather than an object of exposition. It is the unexamined truth against which every other theory is tested, and by the light of which every phenomenon is seen" (*Dematerialisation*, 233). This oversight can be corrected by applying the methods of Theory to Theory. In fact, the problem with Theory is not its supposed relativism and indeterminacy or its proclaimed valorization of diversity and difference but its tendency strategically to abrogate all these principles when they prove inconvenient. The problem with Theory is not its subversiveness but its orthodoxy. As Edward Said, another Theorist who has had second thoughts, notes: "Thus the Marxist reconfirms Marxism, the deconstructionist, deconstruction. One wishes that the whole thing was actually more unsettling, not quite so smug, more likely to get one to forget about one's ideological ties and personal identity in order to think and read differently in novel ways" ("Fantasy's Role," 7).

The Godfather discourse for Theory is Marxism. Though Marxists did not claim that language inherently lacks stable meaning, most American versions of Theory blur any differences between Marxism and Deconstruction by decentering what Theory calls "bourgeois discourse" through deconstructive maneuvers while sliding in its place a very centered Marxist discourse. In practice, the Marxist theory of ideology, the Sartrean theory of "false consciousness," and the deconstructive theory of linguistic instability blend into a single construct used to condemn conservative, liberal, and aesthetic perspectives in literary studies while promoting an academic "progressive" agenda that assumes its own truth and virtue while "interrogating" the motives of all other discourses.

Theory rarely directly advocates communism as it was known in the former USSR; most frequently it gestures vaguely in the direction of Marxist socialism by implied contrast with its attack on the "bourgeois" socioeconomic order. But given the pervasive Marxist ideology that informs Theory and the lack of any clear alternative to the market economy than communism as practiced in the former USSR, North Korea, and so on, I think it reasonable to ask just what Theory has in mind if not the control economy that has proved disastrous wherever attempted.

The New Hegemony is primarily analysis of Theory's theories, but there is an underlying narrative structure: Theory's assumptions emerge from an amalgamation of Deconstruction (chapter 1) and Marxism (chapter 2), and Theory finds its protagonist in a new proletariat composed of its construction of women and racial minorities (chapter 3), disposes of realist fiction and, in fact, reality to make all these constructions credible (chapter 4), and displaces literary and religious discourse so as to usurp their critical power (chapter 5). Additionally chapter 5 argues that there is as much justification for seeing spiritual pathology as the source of political faith as for seeing, as Theory does, political pathology as the source of religious faith.

Some Marxists and feminists have made real contributions to literary thought. Some Populist and radical political ideas point to and offer alternatives to oppressive social and economic practices. What I question is the unreflective academic version of "progressive" thought that sets up rules for other discourses that it cannot hold to in its own. Theory is recognizable in all its variations by its call for political change that "is required to achieve ends that correspond to values that, at another level of theorizing, have been renounced" (Freadman and Miller, 70).

Finally, one habitual motif of Theory, which I have used myself on Theory, is the use of a hypostatized term to sum up, even personify, a variety of practices. Theory does this with "bourgeois," "capitalist," "white male," and the operation all these are said to perform, "oppression." I do it with "Theory," a group term flourished by its proponents, which, as I see it, is a monolithic ideological discourse oppressive to literary study.

THE NEW HEGEMONY
IN LITERARY STUDIES

1

Authorizing Theory

Theory began as an American variant of a French trend of thought and rhetoric, deriving primarily from Jacques Derrida and Michel Foucault. These writers were taken to have proved that what we suppose to be reality, morality, the self, and canonical literature are merely cultural constructions that serve to legitimize an oppressive social order. We suppose that we think our own thoughts, but it is really our oppressive culture's discourse speaking through us, and so on. This set of ideas came along in the early 1970s when American academics were at a height of disillusionment with the official lies used to justify the Vietnam War—as revealed, say, by the Pentagon Papers. So much of the official discourse of this time was *so* insultingly fake and phony that language itself, especially culturally evaluative language, seemed discredited. When Derrida and Foucault put their delegitimizations of language on offer, it is understandable why American academics were ready to buy.

Another of Theory's great advantages was that it was highly useful in helping meet the demand for publication that intensified in American universities in the 1970s. Any initiate who learned the method—and this required little more than learning its vocabulary—could de- and reconstruct language, and, since language constructed "reality," to deconstruct that as well. Derrida and Foucault provided a grid to apply to any text. All texts could be deconstructed into Theory's prescribed pattern and/or unmasked as complicit with "oppression."

Doubtless it helped that Theory was a French export since French sophistication has a cachet for the academically chic. Curiously, however, American academics seem not to realize that Theory became unfashionable in Paris by 1975 (Khilnani, passim). For the most part, Marxist, programmatic anti-Americans and grand theorists were out; liberal conservatives who elaborated and in some cases defended democratic "civil society" were in. Some French protested that most theory was secondhand German thought anyway—a potpourri of Hegel, Nietzsche, Marx, Freud, and Heidegger (Mathy, 273). For a discourse the prestige of which is so clearly dependent on fashion—Theory advocates regularly term those who do

3

not share their faith as "retrograde"—a culture gap so wide seems rather startling. From the current French perspective, Theory is retrograde. Theory has become the dominant discourse only in American English departments, partly because it satisfies a desire for instant all-encompassing condemnations of America and all its ways with no discomfiting qualifications. Theory skyrocketed beyond laborious, empirical (that is, factual) piecemeal critiques of what was wrong with America in the 1970s to the 1990s to an all-embracing assault on the West from Achilles to Agnew, showing evil inherent in Western thought, built even into the structure of language. French method enabled repudiation to become wholesale, to clear the boards of prior authority.

The repudiation of more laborious methods of argument and more nuanced forms of judgment is at least what American academics *read* Derrida and Foucault as saying in some of their more dramatic pronouncements about the "episteme" and "logocentrism." I argue in this chapter that it is not so certain what Derrida and Foucault really meant or, at least, what they would later admit to about what they meant. In fact, many of the central concepts of Theory have proved so unworkable that their supposed authorizers have either indignantly disclaimed or covertly contradicted them. But even those concepts disclaimed by their authors are taken by American progressives as dogma, asserted rather than argued. Most scandalous, there is a contradiction between Theory's professed radical skepticism and its dogmatic reliance on a narrow range of authority figures.

Derrida's Contradictions

Derrida thrilled his American audience by declaring that his methods "already give us the assured means of broaching the deconstruction of *the greatest totality*—the concept of the *episteme* and logocentric metaphysics—within which are produced, without ever posing the radical question of writing, all the Western methods of analysis, explication, reading, or interpretation" (*Of Grammatology,* 46). In "Structure, Sign, and Play in the Discourse of the Human Sciences," his address in the groundbreaking 1970 Johns Hopkins symposium, published as *The Languages of Criticism and the Sciences of Man* (retitled *The Structuralist Controversy* in the influential paperback reissue), Derrida claims the legacy of the most destructive and skeptical modern thought: "the Nietzschean critique of metaphysics, the critique of the concepts of being and truth, for which were substituted the concepts of play, interpretation and sign (sign without truth present); the Freudian critique of self-presence, that is, the critique of consciousness, of the subject, of self-identity and of self-proximity and self-possession; and, more radically, the Heideggerian destruction of metaphysics, of onto-theology, of the determination of being as presence" (250).

Derrida disciples and detractors not unreasonably took this to mean that Derrida claimed to have discredited all "Western" modes of arriving at truth and, just for completeness, had liquidated personal selfhood as well. He is thought to have argued for radical relativism, indeterminacy on both the conceptual and ethical levels, and the malevolence of the Western canon. It could fairly be said that Derrida encouraged such readings by provocative comments such as "I don't believe in perception" (*Structuralist Controversy*, 272) and *"There is nothing outside the text"* (*Of Grammatology*, 158). But this is to miss, at least to some degree, Derrida's qualifications. Some of his most provocative comments are immediately hedged or retroactively abrogated. Thus his authority is frequently cited for ideas he has explicitly repudiated.

For instance, he follows his appropriation of Nietzsche, Freud, and Heidegger with what is, in some respects, a recuperation of the seemingly negated categories of traditional philosophy:

> But all these destructive discourses . . . are trapped in a sort of circle. This circle is unique. It describes the form of the relationship between the history of metaphysics and the destruction of the history of metaphysics. *There is no sense* in doing without the concepts of metaphysics in order to attack metaphysics. We have no language—no syntax and no lexicon—which is alien to this history; we cannot utter a single destructive proposition which has not already slipped into the form, the logic, and the implicit postulates of precisely what it seems to contest. (*Structuralist Controversy*, 250)

It would seem then that Derrida does not claim to have, in one grand gesture, nullified Western thought.

Derrida generally disputes attacks on his supposed positions by denying he ever held them. Thus he cites as stupidity a *New York Times* definition of deconstruction as a theory that "sees in language an integrally false means of expression which always reflects the prejudices of the user" ("Like the Sound of the Deep Sea," 604). In a recent interview he declares, "What is called 'deconstruction' . . . has never opposed institutions as such, philosophy as such, discipline as such." As for the canon, "As soon as one examines my texts, not only mine but the texts of many people close to me, one sees that respect for the great texts, for the texts of the Greeks and of others, too, is the condition of our work" (*Deconstruction*, 5, 9). Most notably, there is the spectacle, the frenzy, of denial in *Limited Incorporated*, which incorporates (to extend Derrida's own pun) his response to the language philosopher John Searle's attack on Derrida's conception of language.

In the afterword to *Limited Incorporated* Derrida clearly goes beyond Searle's specific objections to defend deconstruction generally. Derrida cites an objection frequently made that "since the deconstructionist (which is to say, isn't it, the skeptic-relativist-nihilist!) is supposed not to believe in truth, stability, or the unity of meaning, in intention or 'meaning-to-say,' how can he demand of us that we read *him* with pertinence, rigor?" The answer, he declares, is that "this definition of the deconstructionist is *false* (that's right: false, not true)" (146). Answering a question of his interlocutor, Gerald Graff, he asserts, "I have never 'put such concepts as truth, reference, and the stability of interpretive contexts radically into question' if 'putting radically into question' means contesting that there *are* and that there *should be* truth, reference, and stable concepts of interpretation" (150).

Nor does deconstruction propose indeterminacy: "'deconstruction' should never lead either to relativism or to any sort of indeterminism" (*Limited Incorporated*, 148). Derrida asserts that he has "never assimilated philosophy, science, theory, criticism, law, morality, etc., to literary fictions" (156). This is nice to know, but the problem is that these misconceptions are held by his disciples as well as his enemies and are a major determinant in his American influence. He is taken to have authorized ideas he declares never to have advanced. In fact, the book *Limited Incorporated*, in which he issues the denials above, has on its back cover the blurb that the essays in it "are perhaps the clearest exposition to be found of Derrida's most controversial idea, that linguistic meaning is fundamentally indeterminate." One seems entitled to wonder just how clear Derrida's "clearest exposition" can be. He certainly fooled Johns Hopkins University Press.

In one instance, a characteristic rhetorical maneuver of Derrida, and later, Theory, seems to account for this confusion about what Derrida "really" means. In *Limited Incorporated* Derrida recuperates his frequently derided dictum that "there is nothing outside the text." Derrida is explaining his idea of context: "The phrase which for some has become a sort of slogan, in general so badly understood, of deconstruction ('there is nothing outside the text') means . . . there is nothing outside context. In this form, which says exactly the same thing, the formula would doubtless have been less shocking. I am not certain that it would have provided more to think about" (136). It would not have provided more to think about since it was the very counterintuitiveness and sweeping negation of its supposedly misunderstood use that made it so exciting to American Derrideans.

Though Searle misread Derrida at several points in his "Reiterating the Differences: A Reply to Derrida," he is on the money in a later response:

> The way it works is this: Derrida advances some astounding thesis, for example, writing came before speaking, nothing exists outside of texts, meanings are undecideable. When challenged, he says, "You have misunderstood me, I only meant such and such," where such and such is some well-known platitude. Then when the platitude is acknowledged, he assumes that its acknowledgment constitutes an acceptance of the original exciting thesis. ("Literary Theory," 195)

[An example] is his claim that nothing exists outside texts. (*"Il n'y a pas de hors-texte."*) Here is what he says about it: " *'Il n'y a pas de hors-texte'* means nothing else: there is nothing outside context." So the original preposterous thesis that there is nothing outside of texts is now converted into the platitude that everything exists in some context or other. (196)

The effect is "to achieve the rhetorical effect that might be described as the move from the exciting to the banal and back again" (195). Theory users become famous for counterintuitive, "daring," "transgressory" statements; when those statements are devastatingly refuted they run for cover; when it looks safe again, they sneak back out and reiterate their fallacious flourishes.

Thus when Theory's bold assertions, such as the denial that texts are created by authors, comes under pressure, Theory's version of a miracle occurs, what I shall term the *Lazarus maneuver*, nicely observed by M. H. Abrams:

The author-subject revives . . . divested of quotation marks and other disclaimers, and reinvested with such logocentric, or else bourgeois, attributes as an initiating purpose, a decidable intention to mean what he says, and very human motives and feelings. Or rather, two authors revive. One is the indignant theorist whose views have been described and challenged, and the other is the opponent . . . whom he charges with having misread the obvious meanings of his texts, out of carelessness, or obtuseness, or (it is often implied) for less reputable reasons. (34)

A specific dispute between Searle and Derrida, one especially related to issues of authorship and authority, is about Derrida's supposed denial of intentionality in writing. Searle refutes Derrida's argument that "intentionality is absent from written communication" (*Limited Incorporated*, 201). But this is an instance where Searle has misread. What Derrida proposes in "Signature, Event, Context," the essay in *Limited Incorporated* that provoked Searle's "Reply," is a typology in which "the category of intention will not disappear; it will have its place, but from that place it will no longer be able to govern the entire scene and system of utterance" (18). Indeed, shifting from the ground of language as such to literature, it is evident that Derrida is rather more open to authorial intention than the old "New Critic" William Wimsatt, who coauthored an influential essay, "The Intentional Fallacy," that denied the relevance of authorial intention in determining literary meaning. But there is a crucial difference between Derrida and New Criticism. Whereas New Criticism was ancillary to the author or, as in Wimsatt's case, the text, deconstruction aims at one-upmanship over both, a displacement of author and text by the Theorist. As Derrida puts it, his method "consists in questioning the internal structure of these texts as symptoms" (*Of Grammatology*, 99). In fact, many, if not all, of Derrida's deconstructions are reductive, hardly surprising since their purpose is to exemplify deconstructive method rather than interpret the author. This surely was Derrida's greatest gift to Theory: transferring authority, authorship, from authors to critics.

It is questionable how much we gain from even the most certifiably state-of-the-art deconstructive readings. Exemplary is the essay, "Writing," that Barbara Johnson, an academically honored American deconstructionist Harvard professor, wrote for the University of Chicago Press's introduction to literary theory, *Critical Terms for Literary Study*. She begins by explaining the Derridean doctrine that writing really precedes speech but that all "Western philosophy" privileges speech over writing because speech embodies the myth of presence, "logocentrism" (that is, language as *logos*, Truth divinely endorsed, etc., etc.). But at a certain point in her recitation of the doctrine Johnson clearly runs into a problem:

> While the critique of logocentrism undertaken by Derrida implies that West-ern patriarchal culture has always privileged the presence, immediacy, and ideality of speech over the distance and materiality of writing, this privilege has never, in fact, been unambiguous. An equal but more covert privileging of writing has also been operative. One of the ways in which colonial powers succeeded in imposing their domination over other peoples was precisely through writing. European culture has always seen its own form of literacy as a sign of superiority. The hidden but ineradicable importance of writing that Derrida *uncovers* (my emphasis) in his readings of logocentric texts in fact reflects an unacknowledged or "repressed," *grapho*centrism. It may well be that it is only in a text-centered culture that one can privilege speech in a logocentric way. The "speech" privileged in logocentrism is not literal but is a *figure* of speech: a figure, ultimately, of God. (47)

Johnson's argument is an elephantine dance around a difficulty of its own making. Presenting obvious evidence of the dominating power of writing in West-ern culture, Johnson must explain how this could be when, according to Derrida, that culture is phonocentric, privileging speech. This problem exists only because she preaches the logos of what Derrida "uncovered," a phonocentrism, in fact, not uncovered but invented by him, the historical evidence being that writing has always been massively privileged over speech (see Jackson, *Poverty of Structuralism*, 183–84; and Burke, 135–36). To put it bluntly, in this instance Derrida is wrong. And Johnson's belief in logocentrism is clearly based solely on the argument from authority: that of Derrida. She seems wholly unaware of any other position.

Johnson exemplifies her, or rather Derrida's, oppositional methodology for reading by way of a poem by the seventeenth-century American Puritan Edward Taylor:

Meditation 6

Am I thy gold? Or purse, Lord, for thy wealth,
　　Whether in mine or mint refined for thee?
I'm counted so, but count me o'er thyself,
　　Lest gold washed face, and brass in heart I be.
　　I fear my touchstone touches when I try
　　Me and my counted gold too overly.

Am I new minted by thy stamp indeed?
　　Mine eyes are dim; I cannot clearly see.
Be thou my spectacles that I may read
　　Thine image and inscription stamped on me.
　　If thy bright image do upon me stand,
　　I am a golden angel in thy hand.

Lord, make my soul thy plate, thine image bright
　　Within the circle of the same enfile.
And on its brims in golden letters write
　　Thy superscription in an holy style.
　　Then I shall be thy money, thou my horde:
　　Let me thy angel be, be thou my Lord.
　　　　　　　　　　(43–44)

Johnson starts out well, noting the extended metaphor of gold coinage as spiritual value, as instanced in the pun on "angel" as both a heavenly being and a seventeenth-century coin. She sees that the poem questions how to interpret signs. But her reading seems to me rather thin, ultimately forcing the poem into obedience to her (Derrida's) system. I will pick up partway through her appropriation:

The gold begins to resemble a sign, with no guaranteed correlation between face (signifier) and heart (signified). The becoming sign process continues in the second stanza, where the speaker is "stamped" with an image and an inscription. The speaker is now a reader, and what he reads is himself. God has become an image, and a corrective lens. In the final stanza, the text ("inscription") that was dimly decipherable in the second stanza turns out not yet to have been written. While the poem still yearns for a perfectly reciprocal container/contained relation ("I shall be thy money, thou my horde"), this relation now requires the active intervention of writing ("In golden letters write / Thy superscription"). In his increasingly aggressive submissiveness, the speaker tries to order God to take his place as the writer. (44)

This is a good account of the poem except for missing the complications of some important images as they relate to the extended metaphor of coinage/value and, I will argue, failing to recognize the complications of the operation of Grace, the poem's main argument.

As I read it, the poem goes like this: Stanza 1: A Calvinist knows that Grace cannot be assured by works, in the biblical sense, still less by social reputation. What looks outwardly like gold may be merely a wash, that is, "a solution applied to metals for producing an appearance of gold or silver [first usage, 1697]" (*The Shorter Oxford English Dictionary on Historical Principles* [2388]). If uncertain, one might try the coin with a touchstone, "a smooth, fine-grained . . . variety of quartz or jasper . . . used for testing the quality of gold and silver alloys by the colour of the streak produced by rubbing them upon it [1530]" (2219). The problem is that the touchstone might "try," that is, "endeavor to ascertain by experiment [1573]" but also "to separate (metal) from the ore or dross by melting; to refine, purify by fire [1686]" (2258) the metal too "overly," that is, "on the surface [1573]" (1404), superficially.

Stanza 2: One can only be in the image of God through Grace, rebirth, a new minting authenticated by the seal of God, equivalent to the image of the monarch on coinage. But how can one determine Grace, except through perception enabled by Grace, since original sin dims our vision? So God's Grace becomes the spectacles through which his seal of value can be read.

Stanza 3: So the speaker prays—the imperative form in prayer is not unusual—for God to enfile, that is, inscribe, His image on the speaker's soul, imaged as "plate," "a thin piece of silver or gold" (1519). God's superscription will authenticate the speaker as an angel, part of God's wealth while God's Grace will be the speaker's wealth, his mark of authenticity. As we say, it is a win-win situation, though, as is inherent in the prayer form, a proleptic one.

One may object that I have centered the meaning of the poem, disregarding what Derrida calls the "freeplay" (*jeu*) of its signifiers. Perhaps so, but no more than Johnson does. The difference is that I read the poem as centered on God's authentication and she on Derrida's. God's authority may be Taylor's myth, but Derrida's conception of phono- and logocentricity is Johnson's myth. Indeed, my reading does not depend on belief in God though it assumes Taylor's writing did. Johnson's reading, however, depends on belief in Derrida, in the Logos of Logocentricity.

Johnson's essay may be less literary criticism than performance of a rite, affirming yet again, with all the redundancy of true believers, her version of "Thy [Derrida's] superscription in an holy style." It reduces Taylor's historical and religious "difference" to contemporary orthodoxy, tautologically reading the poem as an allegory of the very opposition between writing and speech that deconstruction axiomatically assumes. Taylor illustrates Derrida and Johnson, but Derrida and Johnson do not illuminate Taylor. The historical tensions in Taylor's poem, expressing Calvinistic rather than Derridean oppositions, go unnoticed. Neither critic nor reader can discover anything they did not "always already" know.

There is, then, a serious problem regarding author, authority, and authorization in Deconstruction. Vincent Descombes remarks that Theory is "a critique of authority in which, from the terms of the critique itself, what is at once presumed and indefensible is the authority of the critique" (cited in Prendergast, 245). The very term "Derridean," as with "Althusserian" and "Foucauldian," gives away the game of a discourse that sometimes claims (as we have seen, Derrida, at least sometimes disclaims as well) to have deconstructed not only authority but authors. Big names in Theory function less as conceptual markers than as totems and fetishes that inspire participation mystique in the believers and can be waved intimidatingly at the uninitiated. Theorists, some of whom (though not Derrida) excoriate the literary "canon" for its malign cultural authority, have themselves replaced it.

The question of authority over the text is interestingly addressed in the Derrida/Searle exchange. Derrida's *Limited Incorporated* and his afterword to that work are deconstructible as a claim for authority over both his *and* Searle's texts, and the anxiety and fury Derrida claims to find in Searle are actually projected from his own response to Searle's challenge to his authority. Derrida quotes the passage in Searle that evidently most upset him, with a revealing parenthetical interruption: "Derrida has a distressing [why distressing? for whom?] penchant for saying things that are obviously false" (*Limited Incorporated*, 80). Derrida finds it strange that anyone should be distressed by what they take to be obvious falsehoods. It is strange that he finds this strange. In some instances, as previously noted, Searle does misunderstand Derrida—almost as badly as Derrideans do. But in the central instance of phono- and logocentrism, Derrida's claims are provably false (to quote Derrida on Searle, *"false* [that's right: false, not true"] (*Limited Incorporated*, 146).

The more interesting question, however, is not which of these writers is correct on a given point but the degree of Derrida's anxiety about a tough but not uncommon accusation in scholarly writing. Derrida asserts that Searle "has an anxiety and compulsion to stamp and seal the truth" and that "his confidence in the truth he claims to possess is a poor front for considerable uneasiness" (*Limited Incorporated*, 30). He describes Searle as "passionate and exacerbated" (41), as only able to read Derrida "feverishly" (42), and claims that Searle's procedure is "to insult an author instead of criticizing him through demonstration" (139). Whose anxiety, compulsion, uneasiness, passion, exacerbation, feverishness, and insults is this really about?

One of Derrida's strategies is to deride Searle for copyrighting his "Reply," claiming this as evidence of Searle's anxiety over "his rights as an author," that "these rights might be questioned, that someone might try to steal them from him," that his work might "be expropriated, alienated" (*Limited Incorporated*, 30). Derrida attempts just such expropriation by quoting *all* of Searle's essay within his own. He ridicules copyright as a philosophically futile attempt to *own* one's writing, to protect it from shifting readings, interpretation, critique. Moreover, by Searle's naming D. Searle and H. Dreyfus as having influenced his ideas, Derrida argues that Searle gives away how little his discourse, or anyone's, is solely individual rather than corporate. He then insults Searle by renaming him Sarl, the French abbreviation for *Société à responsabilité limitée*, that is, a corporation with limited liability.

Derrida virtuously waives his own rights to his writing, given that such rights depend on evidently onerous police powers: "I will not claim the copyright because ultimately there is always a police and a tribunal ready to intervene each time that a rule . . . is invoked in a case involving signatures" (*Limited Incorporated*, 105). The effect of this grand gesture is somewhat nullified when, in the same volume that contains "Limited a b c," Derrida does copyright his afterword. Worse yet, Derrida cuts and runs when Gerald Graff questions his seeming "to say that any specification of linguistic rules and contexts plays into the hands of the police, or that there is something politically suspect in the very project of attempting to fix the contexts of utterances" (131). Derrida responds by denying any intention to represent "the law, the tribunal or the police as political powers *repressive in themselves*" (132).

At any rate, it is Derrida who is the police here, he who is obsessed, as he accuses Searle of being, with the "procedure of inheritance and of legitimation" (*Limited Incorporated*, 42). No one refers to "Searlean" theory nor attempts to "demonstrate" an interpretation by appealing to Searle's authority. Derrida's anxiety toward Searle's "Reply" is not so odd if we see Derrida as defending an institutional discursive authority, Derridean thought. A corporation might similarly sue to protect its logo if not logos. There may even be a precapitalist mode of response encoded into *Limited Incorporated*. Searle committed not merely authority infringement but *lèse-majesté*.

Foucault's Contradictions

Contradictions relating to authority are not peculiar to Derrida but endemic to Theory. This is especially the case with Foucault, an even greater influence than Derrida on American literary studies though Foucault did not so much displace Derrida as become merged with him in the construction of Theory. Logocentrism was melted into Foucault's ruling terms, "episteme" and "discourse." These served the same purpose of enabling a blanket condemnation of the West but with the apparent advantages of greater historical specificity and a less predictable method of reading. Moreover, Foucault's attack on Western humanism was even less qualified than Derrida's, though not without flagrant contradictions, particularly between his influential histories of "discourses" and his later essays and interviews. So besides the question of why Foucault should be taken as an authority, there is that of which Foucault is the authority. Does the later Foucault get to overrule the earlier? Theory generally solves this problem by ignoring it.

Foucault was first celebrated for identifying, in *The Order of Things*, the successive underlying modes of awareness for all Western thought, what he called "epistemes." Each mode determined what was possible to think during its era and was discontinuous with the preceding and succeeding mode. The term soon proved so overgeneralized, totalistic, and vacuous as to be useless. As Erik Midelfort noted, "We will have to work with structures of mind that do not pretend to underlie all of the thinking, or even all of the best thinking, of an age. There is too much diversity in any one period, and too much continuity between periods, for the relentless quest for the elusive *episteme* to prove ultimately useful" (259). As "episteme" became an embarrassment, Foucault and more sophisticated Foucauldians silently dropped it—it does not rate an index citation in Lentricchia and McLaughlin's *Critical Terms*, even though Paul Bové's chapter on "Discourse" centers on Foucault—in favor of the slightly more modest term "discursive formations."

What Foucault defines as "discourse" replaces reality and experience: "What, in short, we wish to do is dispense with 'things.' To 'derepresentify' them. . . . To substitute for the enigmatic treasure of 'things' anterior to discourse, the regular formation of objects that emerge only in discourse" (*Archeology*, 47). A "thing," such as mental illness, is "constituted by all that was said in all the statements that named it, divided it up . . . judged it, and possibly gave it speech by articulating in its name, discourses that were to be taken as its own" (32). "We no longer relate discourse to the primary ground of experience, nor to the *a priori* authority of knowledge; but we seek the rules of its formation in discourse itself" (79).

As with Derrida, Foucault seems to clear the board. Yet Foucault turned out to be even less a Foucauldian than Derrida is a Derridean. For instance, Foucauldianism appeals to Foucault's authority but fails to note Foucault's abjurations against political moralizing. In *Order* Foucault expresses scorn at "those who in their profound stupidity, assert there is no philosophy without political choice, that all thought is either 'progressive' or 'reactionary'" (328). In *Archeology* he denies that one can make blanket accusations of ideology: "Few discourses have given so much place to ideology as clinical discourse or that of political economy: that is not a sufficiently good reason to treat the totality of their statements as being undermined by error, contradiction, and a lack of objectivity" (186). In *Power/Knowledge* he notes the lack of specific analysis of fascism that "enables fascism to be used as a floating signifier, whose function is essentially that of denunciation. The procedures of every form of power are suspected of being facets" (139). Yet these instances of what Foucault called "profound stupidity" are basic to literary Foucauldianism.

Foucauldians also routinely ignore their founder's injunctions against total-ization: "Nothing would be more false than to see in the analysis of discursive for-mations an attempt at totalitarian periodization, whereby from a certain moment and for a certain time, everyone would think in the same way, in spite of surface differences, say the same thing through a polymorphous vocabulary, and produce a sort of great discourse that one could travel over in any direction" (Foucault, *Archeology*, 148). But Foucauldian denunciations of Western, humanist, white male discourse assume just such a totalitarian periodization. Foucault attacks critics who regard his work "as an enterprise whose aim is to discover cultural totalities, to homogenize the most obvious differences, and to rediscover the universality of constrictive forms" (204). But these distortions *are* Foucauldianism.

Some of these problems stem from contradictions within Foucault as well as between Foucault and Foucauldianism. For one, what makes his discourse on discourse any more authoritative than those he, as Foucaldians say, "interrogates"? In *Archeology*, Foucault uneasily admits that "for the moment, and as far ahead as I can see, my discourse, far from determining the locus in which it speaks, is avoiding the ground on which it could find support" (204). But admission of self-privileging is not justification for it. As J. G. Merquior notes, "Foucault does not give up at least one truth claim: that his own analytics of power is true" (146).

Like Derrida, Foucault is always showing that the "real" meanings of what the "bourgeois" say are different, even opposite, to what they think they mean. This is what John McGowan calls "interpreter's privilege": "Interpretive theory must . . . justify claims that would not meet with the agent's consent, an undertaking that always involves privileging the observers' account over the agents" (49). Foucault's authority in his construction of "discursive formations" depends on "interpreter's privilege," which he and other Theorists *assume* without explaining how they at-tained it, thus swinging on the branch they have sawed off.

Though Foucault disclaimed any totalizing theory, such a theory does surface in the book that most denies its possibility, *Archaeology*. It is the Marxist principle of contradiction. Foucault asserts that at the end of his mode of analysis: "The fundamental contradiction emerges: the bringing into play, at the very origin of the system, of incompatible postulates. . . . Such a contradiction, far from being an appearance or accident of discourse, far from being that from which it must be freed if its truth is at last to be revealed, constitutes the very law of its existence" (150–51). A Theorist might claim that Foucault's use of contradiction is dialectical and thus evades totality and foundation. But this alibi is brilliantly refuted by a philosopher who doubts that "the meager logic of contradiction" can "actually serve as a principle of intelligibility and rule of action in political struggle" and abjures that "one must try to think struggle and its forms, objectives, means and processes in terms of a logic free of the sterilising constraints of the dialectic." This philosopher is Foucault (*Power/Knowledge*, 143–44).

Yet *Power/Knowledge* recuperates another totalizing term, the notorious "Gaze." The Gaze was originally formulated in Jean-Paul Sartre's *Being and Nothingness*, elaborated in Frantz Fanon's anticolonial theory, and became a major category of feminist film criticism. It is the shaming, intimidating gaze of the oppressor at the oppressed. Foucault posits the Gaze as a more efficient form of tyranny than more overt forms of violence:

> In contrast [to overt violence] you have the system of surveillance, which on the contrary involves very little expense. There is no need for arms, physical violence, material constraints. Just a gaze. An inspecting gaze, a gaze which each individual under its weight will end by interiorising to the point that he is his own overseer, each individual thus exercising this surveillance over and against himself. (155; the entire essay, "The Eye of Power," is relevant)

Foucault's specific histories of the "discourses" of madness, the clinic, and prisons center on surveillance, the Gaze. Obviously, the effect of Foucault's analysis of the gaze depends on our seeing it as an immoral form of power. Yet Foucault adheres to Nietzsche's analysis in *Genealogy of Morals* of any notion of morality being always already a self-interested mask for power seeking. If power is all there is, if all forms of "knowledge," including ethical judgment, are really impositions of power (*Power/Knowledge*, passim), and if "for modern thought, no morality is possible" (*Power/Knowledge*, 328), then what is *wrong* with the form of power embodied in the Gaze or any other form of power?

There is a more serious difficulty: Can Foucault make good on the specific historical instances of the tyranny of surveillance, the domination of the Gaze? Foucault's histories derive their grand syntheses on the basis of anecdotal "evidence" at best, pure fiction at worst. The New Historicist version of Theory, derived from Foucault, quite openly bases large generalizations on isolated anecdotes. Indeed, Heather Dubrow valorizes "the Foucauldian anecdote" in her introduction to a *PMLA* special issue on "The Status of Evidence" (13–14). She includes in the issue a distinguished roundtable panel that considers the anecdote as a central mode of "progressive" evidence (25–26). Barbara Riebling lacks Dubrow's simple faith: "Bluntly, we need more than the idle assertion that power is 'everywhere and nowhere,' paired with a few great anecdotes" (191).

An extraordinary anecdote centers the first chapter of *Madness and Civilization*, "Stultifera Navis." Foucault argues that the medieval order was inclusive of the mad and that it was enlightenment humanism that brutalized them. Foucault cites late medieval literary tales of the ship of fools (*stultifera navis, narrenschiff*) as exemplary of the free circulation of the medieval mad, asserting that "they did exist, these boats that conveyed their insane cargo from town to town." After citing instances, he arrestingly concludes, "Often the cities of Europe must have seen these 'ships of fools' approaching their harbors" (8). This is a wonderful story except that Erik Midelfort, after searching the archives for confirmation of Foucault's assertions, found *no* evidence for ships of fools outside the fictional uses of art and literature (Midelfort, 254).

One of Foucault's most influential works, *Discipline and Punish*, is anecdotally centered on Jeremy Bentham's design for a circular prison with optimum scope for the Gaze, the Panopticon. Foucault asserts that "in the 1830s the Panopticon became the architectural programme of most prison projects" (249). But the fact is that, as Bentham complained, the authorities showed little interest in the Panopticon. Richard Hamilton notes that the government preferred sending prisoners to Australia: "Power, it appears, was not interested in surveillance. Power preferred those prisoners to be far away; it wished them to be entirely out of sight" (176). The problem is not just in the anecdotes; in several of his books Foucault gets entire eras wrong. Roy Porter's careful historical study, *Mind-Forg'd Manacles*, proves that to the degree that there was a "Great Confinement" of the mentally ill it came about in the nineteenth century, not the Enlightenment, as Foucault claimed in *Madness* (Porter, 5–9). Moreover, in England there was a diversity of views toward and treatments of the mad rather than the Foucauldian One Big Paradigm (111).

What needs rethinking about Foucault, however, is not only his specific historical blunders but the cogency of the paranoiac philosophical perspective that dominates his work and characterizes New Historicism. This problem is strongly addressed in Lawrence Stone's review essay, "Madness," and the interesting exchange between Foucault and Stone that followed. Stone protests not only that "[Foucault's] dark vision of modern society . . . accords with only some of the historical facts" (30) but also against the general reductiveness of Foucault and the Foucauldians: "It is one thing to overthrow the simplistic Whig interpretation [of ongoing progress in human affairs], but another to put in its place an equally simplistic pessimism that seems unable to distinguish antibiotics or insulin from charms, prayers, or whips" (36).

Foucault responded to this not unusually critical reading with a fury similar to Derrida's at Searle (Foucault, "An Exchange"). This was a tactical error for it enabled Stone to respond by raising the central issue in Foucauldian discourse, Foucault's "'dominance and control' model of human relationships" which Stone observes is "a model so all-embracing as to be virtually meaningless. It can include anything from forced labor in the Gulag Archipelago to teaching children to brush their teeth" ("An Exchange," 44). Indeed, a celebrated New Historicist essay by Richard Brodhead, "Sparing the Rod: Discipline and Fiction," applies Foucault point for point in showing how nineteenth-century Americans brought up their children "in what Foucault calls the disciplinary archipelago" by brainwashing them into making "the *self* the governor of the self" (162). Brodhead presents his demonization of self-control as an urgent political message. Does he really suppose that the major danger to American children today is *too much self-control?*

How cogent are Foucauldian views of the United States as a surveillance society? It is true that a few Panopticon-like prison structures were built in the United States, but the panopticon was not the dominant design. Richard Hamilton notes that Hollywood prison movies are more accurate. What I think is a great prison film, Jules Dassin's *Brute Force*, depicts a prison built on a rectangular cell block plan. This accords with what Richard Hamilton shows is the dominant prison design as against the panopticon: "There is no observation tower; there is no central, continuous surveillance. In fact, except for the occasional guard on patrol, no one is in a position to observe the prisoners in the manner alleged by Foucault. Moreover, few hospitals, factories, schools, or barracks are based on the Bentham plan. In this case an entire school of 'social history' has been built on a patent nonfact" (178). In *Brute Force* the guards have little control over the prisoners' violence toward one another, one of the *actual* scandals of American prisons where homosexual rape and effectual gang control of prisoners' lives are commonplace. One can learn more about American prisons from films such as *Brute Force* and *American Me* than from Foucault's *Discipline and Punish.*

Foucault conflates carceral and surveillance societies. A strong case could be made for America as a carceral and punitive society simply by citing execution and prison population statistics, but the notion that the United States is a surveillance society needs more evidence than citing Foucault and selected anecdotes. The case ignores American mobility and distances. Nowhere in the West is it easier to disappear and resurface with a newly manufactured identity than in America, there being far less *state* or *social* surveillance than in most European countries. Foucauldian surveillance applies far more clearly to the Second World of the former Soviet Union and China than to the First, *as Foucault later admitted* when he attacked the French Left for "universalizing dissolutions [of the Soviet Gulag] into *the general form of internment*" (*Power/Knowledge*, 137; my emphasis), evidently without recognizing how much such a strategy depended on Foucauldianism.

What then accounts for Foucault's great authority, especially in American English departments? In the face of his philosophical contradictions and his gross and astonishing historical errors, how can such an intelligent and sophisticated critic as Paul Bové pronounce authoritatively that Foucault "has *shown* [my emphasis] how [discourse] works in the case of prisons and medical clinics" (57)? Evidently Theory cannot dispense with the totalism of Foucauldian discourse, which claims to undermine all other modes of discourse by simply showing them as oppressive by virtue of being discourse. But how then is Foucauldian discourse not oppressive?

Emily Weinauer's essay, "Plagiarism and the Proprietary Self: Policing the Boundaries of Authorship in Herman Melville's 'Hawthorne and His Mosses,'" is a case in point. Weinauer argues that Melville "attempts to unsettle—then finally reinscribes" the notion of the writer as owner of the text, which itself reflects what C. B. Macpherson calls "possessive individualism," the notion of the individual as owner of his or her self. In this context the superior political correctness of plagiarism is celebrated: "The cornerstone of the theory of possessive individualism is Locke's assertion that the self is ratified by the property that it acquires through labor. Hence the disruption of subjectivity accomplished by the act of plagiarism: as the plagiarist unsettles the relationship between an original author and his or her text, he or she contests the very selfhood of the no-longer-possessing author" (698). The relation of author to text is like that of parent to child and master to slave: "Posing as an originator, the plagiarist unmakes old affiliations and creates new ones, giving the child a new parent, the slave a new master, the text a new author. By breaking the law, in short, the plagiarist disrupts the field of significations that the law sets in place, disputing claims of legitimacy and natural authority" (701). Though Melville does somewhat unsettle authorial proprietorship, and thus personal selfhood, "ultimately fear wins out: try as he may, Melville cannot escape the desire to keep the boundaries of that subject sovereign, secure from plagiaristic theft" (702).

This essay is less interesting for what it says about Melville than what it shows about Foucauldian foundationalism—Foucault's "What Is an Author?" is, Weinauer says, her "foundational text" (715). Once Foucauldianism plus a dash of Macpherson is gridded onto Melville, the essay is perfectly predictable, redundant even if true: Theory taught us long ago that all canonical American writers were guilty of possessive individualism, so such Foucauldian painting by numbers is superfluous.

The essay does become politically relevant if we do a Foucauldian deconstruction of it. This is not to say the essay is totally self-contradictory. Arguably it is a kind of plagiarism of Foucauldianism, an example of communal thinking, thus politically correct from Weinauer's perspective. But does not Weinauer's essay also ratify her political self, which is *her* center of selfhood, through its labor? The implicit binary opposition is of Melville's imperfect political rectitude as against Weinauer's political perfection, proven by the rigor of her gaze at Melville. Surely Weinauer's political identity affirmation works as a claim to professional legitimacy within her discursive formation. Indeed, it could be argued that she is, to use her comparison, enslaving Melville's writing, appropriating it to define her political, professional selfhood.

Finally, the essay illustrates another Foucauldian paradox: that the easiest site on which to find the Gaze is in the Foucauldian essay that puts a nineteenth-century writer under surveillance and finds him deviant in relation to the disciplinary discursive standards of 1997. Weinauer *is* the police. The discursive site of the contemporary panopticon seems to be the English department.

There is still, however, a mystery about Foucault's particular authority, the authority accorded his own writing. Finally, I think it can be explained only as a case of Real Authorial Presence, a basic though not admitted Theory doctrine. Foucault's explanation of the author function "as the unifying principle in a particular group of writings or statements, lying at the origins of their significance, as the seat of their coherence" (*Archeology*, 221) applies to no contemporary author so well as Foucault himself.

Particularly interesting is Foucault's observation of a historical shift in authorization: In medieval discourse it was "indispensable that a scientific text be attributed to an author, for the author was the index of the work's truthfulness. A proposition was held to derive its scientific value from its author" (*Archeology*, 222–23). But now literary writing privileges personal authorship, whereas scientific disciplines "are defined by groups of objects, methods, their corpus of propositions considered to be true, the interplay of rules and definitions, of techniques and tools: all these constitute a sort of anonymous system, freely available to whoever is able to make use of them, without there being any question of their meaning or their validity being derived from whoever happened to invent them" (222). Foucault's discourse works in American universities as a literary and religious mode of authorship disguised as a scientific one. Foucauldian critics are empowered by communally sharing in Foucauldian presence. There is a book on Foucault entitled *Saint Foucault.*

In *Archeology* Foucault asks, who is "qualified" to speak an authoritative discourse: "Who derives from it his own special quality, his prestige, and from whom, in return, does he receive, if not the assurance, at least the presumption that what he says is true? What is the status of the individuals who—alone—have the right . . . to proffer such a discourse?" (50). It is my argument that Theory works less as a traditional academic discourse than what Foucault terms "doctrinal discourse": "Doctrine involves the utterance of speakers in the sense that doctrine is, permanently, the sign, the manifestation and the instrument of a prior adherence—adherence to a class, to a social or racial status, to a nationality or an interest, to a struggle, a revolt, resistance or acceptance. Doctrine links individuals to certain types of utterance while consequently barring them from all others" (*Archeology*, 226). The interpretive community authorized by Foucault, one which has predictably the same things to say of the West, of market societies, and of white males, thus works in much the same fashion to limit the proliferation of critical discourse that Foucault attributes to the author of fiction: It "impedes the free circulation, the free manipulation, the free composition, decomposition, and recomposition of fiction" ("What Is an Author?" 159).

The Problem with Theory

Theory is full of air pockets. It seems odd that a discourse that so professes skepticism, suspicion, and, above all, diversity, has authorized, after searching through all twentieth-century thought, only one political scientist, one philosopher, one "historian," and one psychologist: the discursive law firm of Althusser, Derrida, Foucault, and Lacan (not included in this analysis because he is merely a variant of the same themes). And authorized these Masters of the (Academic) Universe surely are. In text after text of Theory they are said to have *demonstrated* or *shown* what an accurate perspective would describe as what they asserted, frequently with the flimsiest of arguments and with total disregard for evidence. If the post-structuralist grand masters are read as dogma, it may be because this is all they have to offer. Derrida's doctrines are falsifiable, as are Foucault's particular historical epistemes. Althusser's politics have never liberated a prisoner of thought, and Lacan's psychology is not known for its healing of troubled minds. Yet these thinkers represent Philosophy, History, Politics, and Psychology for Theory and to cite them is to prove oneself "interdisciplinary." The worst aspect of Theory is its illustration of the intellectual version of Gresham's Law, bad thinking driving out good. And as we have seen, Theory rests not on the authority of empirical evidence or on logical argument, certainly not on the tradition it so despises, but primarily on an authority constituted by self-privileging and self-contradiction.

Yet while Derrida *et cie* gave Theory its weaponry for a sweeping negation of Western thought, Theory needed its own positive plotline and a heroic protagonist. The next two chapters describe how Theory developed its plot and its characters.

2

Marxist Utopianism

The Fall and Rise of Marxist Ideology

Deconstruction had inherent problems as a long-range critical methodology. Although the deconstructive method could be applied to an infinite number of texts, its tautological routines became increasingly predictable. If you knew the text and knew the method, everything past the first paragraph was superfluous, grid work. What finally was the point of proving yet again that language pointed only to itself and that Western logic was self-contradictory? To survive, deconstruction needed to mutate, to find a new form that allowed content with some emotive resonance.

Another of the group of discourses that became major components of Theory, Marxism, was also facing difficulties, even before the collapse of the USSR. Indeed, the original French impulse toward Theory came from the need to find a substitute for the discredited authority of the French Communist Party. After the debacle of the abortive revolution of May 1968, when neither the French Communist Party nor the working classes came to the support of the student rioters, French intellectuals backed off from outright communist allegiance while still incorporating the Western Marxist critique of capitalist ideology into an even more linguistically oriented mode: "Free the Signifier!" replaced "Storm the Barricades!"

But in an extraordinary development, these two discourses came to each other's rescue in America. Marxist socialism, *allied* with deconstruction, became part of the hegemonic discourse of major English and history departments in the very country in which Marxism had the least roots, that is, the United States. (In England the same conjunction occurred but in reverse order: Marxism was "the parent culture onto which post-structuralism became grafted" [Easthope, 2].) This chapter shows some problems, mainly of omission, in Theory's critique of "capitalist," "Western" ideology as conceived from the perspective of Marxist socialist ideology.

Initially there was alarm at the "fall" of the USSR among American progressives. Gerald Graff lamented "a cultural situation in which being 'Left' and 'radical' no longer necessarily means being socialist or anti-capitalist. With the decline of socialism as a realistic social alternative, the Left no longer possesses a shared criterion for evaluating cultural phenomena as historically progressive or regressive" (173).

Richard Ohmann, though acknowledging that "whatever historical allowances we made," the formerly communist regimes were "deformed alternatives, betrayals or failures of an idea, false utopias," similarly mourns "the stunning collapse of the socialist project": "What will the world be like without any living alternative to capitalism? . . . What can the idea of socialism amount to if nobody is trying to enact it?" (236). In fact, Theory has done quite well at maintaining not so much the socialist idea as its *ideal*, far less of a problem. Theory has found a way to valorize socialism without needing to defend actual socialist performance, and mechanically "evaluating cultural phenomena as historically progressive or regressive" has become a main activity of English departments. Ohmann declares the need to "invent a new narrative": "English . . . would seem a natural place for the utopian impulse to range" (237). This chapter shows how the socialist utopian impulse extended its range by means of strategic omission and the flourish of political righteousness.

The Critical Unconscious

Marxism's historical problem is nicely framed by Milan Kundera: "Communists used to believe that in the course of capitalist development the proletariat would gradually grow poorer and poorer, but when it finally became clear that all over Europe workers were driving to work in their own cars, they felt like shouting that reality was deceiving them. Reality was stronger than ideology" (*Immortality*, 114). Theory elaborated three discursive devices for surmounting this difficulty.

The first was, as Ohmann called for, to invent a new narrative, the content of which is a representation of women and of minority groups as a new proletariat—the subject of the next chapter, "Visible Saints."

The second was to shift from economics to culture as the playground of "critical theory" (the term favored by academic Marxists for what they call their "project"). Theory found it convenient to follow the "Western Marxism" of Jean-Paul Sartre, Louis Althusser, Theodore Adorno, and others, which centers on ideology, on *cultural* politics, rather than economics or *political* politics: "Western Marxism got quite good at explaining Schonberg or Joyce. But it never explained why the Communist countries could not feed themselves, and the capitalist ones had a food surplus" (Jackson, *Dematerialisation*, 145). But while some Western Marxists valued high culture as a form of resistance to capitalist hegemony, though inevitably compromised and ambiguous, Theory's twist was a wholesale denigration of all "bourgeois humanist Western culture" in contrast to the self-evidence of Critical Theory, that is, their own discourse. We shall see in this and succeeding chapters how Theory pulled off this coup through the concept of ideology.

The third maneuver, *the mysterious missing comparison,* is its most effective—and necessary—device. It can be seen in the following passage from Philip Brian Harper's *Framing the Margins,* which examines the encounter between Ralph Ellison's Invisible Man and a young man symbolically named Emerson. Emerson has just exclaimed, "Identity! My God! Who has identity any more anyway?"

> We might say that Emerson is an emblem of the twentieth century crisis of the individual, whose integrity of identity has been threatened by the increasingly rationalized mode of production that characterizes industrial capitalism in the era. In his exclamation to the protagonist, however, Emerson posits as inevitable the forces that confront the individual in search of identity. With their actual basis in capitalist production thus veiled, mystified, these now apparently natural forces seem to offer an intangible foe to be confronted by the Invisible Man in a metaphysical quest for individual identity. (121–22)

It is interesting what the passage itself posits as self-evident in blaming "capitalist production" for the rationalization of work and the supposed resultant loss of individuality. Harper uses the noun phrase "capitalist production" to simplify the diverse actualities of the marketplace into a single, clearly definable demonic process. Harper's paralogism is what philosophers call "hypostatization" and Marxists—when they attribute it to their opponents—"reification"; that is, "Capital" becomes a "supraindividual entity mysteriously endowed with powers to act" (Elster, 191). In fact, "Capital" is to Marxists what Satan is to some Christians, an embodiment of Evil.

But what is most odd and most typical of the passage is the *mysterious missing comparison,* which works as what poststructuralists call an "aporia" and Marxists themselves a "contradiction," that is, a significant omission that by its very absent presence reveals both an ideological dilemma and the attempt to cover it up. Harper indicts "Capitalism" not for this or that reformable injustice or error in its temporary historical operations but *as a system,* a critique that is inchoate unless some other system could be seen as an alternative. What could this be? It seems unlikely that Harper wishes a return to hunting and gathering, subsistence agriculture, or feudalism.

"Capitalism" in Theory usually operates in a sociopolitical void. The demonizing reification, the absence of clear definition, and the taking for granted of "capitalism" as an unquestionable evil are classic hegemonic procedures. A useful aspect of this rhetoric is that while attacking capitalist ideology, one does not have to defend *or even name* the alternative to it that is the absent presence of the discourse. There is, of course, an alternative system, yet never in Harper's index do the words "communism" or even "socialism" appear, though Harper cites such communist thinkers as Marx, Lukacs, Gramsci, and Jameson. Could this be the love that dare not speak its name?

While Theory uses Marxist categories to "interrogate" the American social, economic, and political world, the performances of present and past Marxist socialist regimes are not brought in for comparison. Comparisons are made not between the brutal realities of capitalism and the (more) brutal realities of Marxist socialism but between the brutal realities of capitalism and the implicit ideals of socialism. Marxist concepts are used to critique "capitalism" but democratic and capitalist concepts are not used to critique really existing socialism. One evidently thinks *with* Marxism but never *about* it. Of course, some progressives deny that Marxism was perfectly realized in real-world communist societies. But neither has Adam Smith's ideal of capitalism been apparent in actual capitalist society. Thus a symmetrical comparison would be between Marx and Smith, not Marx and United Fruit.

How significant omission operates is explainable in Marxist terms. Pierre Macherey theorizes that "it seems useful and legitimate to ask of every production what it tacitly implies, what it does not say." In any work or indeed discursive formation "to say anything, there are certain things *which must not be said*" (85). The true task of criticism is to interpret *"the unconscious of the work"* (92), "the unconscious which is history, the play of history beyond its edges, encroaching on those edges: this is why it is possible to trace the path which leads from the haunted work to that which haunts it" (94). Marxist criticism is haunted by Marxist socialist practice. By limiting its discourse to capitalism, Theory illustrates Macherey's contention that "the unspoken has many other resources: it assigns speech to its exact position, designating its domain. By speech, silence becomes the centre and principle of expression, its vanishing point. Speech eventually has nothing more to tell us: we investigate the silence, for it is the silence that is doing the speaking" (86).

I propose to say things *which must not be said*, first, by using Marxist critical methods on Marxist criticism and, second, by supplementing Marxism with the silenced critiques *of* it, thus introducing a comparative and dialogic element into the closed circle of hegemonical discourse. I shall therefore cite the analyses of the former Polish Marxist insider Leszek Kolakowski, as well as the informed analyses of Jon Elster, Peter L. Berger, Alvin Gouldner, Richard Pipes, and others. True, as Constable Dogberry detected, comparisons are odorous. Theory prefers to cite the most awful aspects of "capitalism" in an implied comparison to an ideal utopia. For not only are comparisons odorous but, as Kundera observed, so is reality. Here is where poststructuralism proves so useful by banishing the inconveniences of reality, the troublesome historical record, with a wave of its deconstructive wand.

If "reality" is merely a verbal construction, just verbally reconstruct it; no reality, no problem with it.

What makes the absolute, the ideal, and the a priori so wonderful is that they are *in*comparable. One of the most noted aspects of Marxism is the lack of what sociologist Robert Merton calls "'theories of the middle range'" (cited in Elster, 14). Lenin, in his attack on trade unionism, declared there was "'no middle course'" between bourgeois society and socialism (Kolakowski, 2:387). This absolutist, all-or-nothing perspective seems a trait of Theory in all its forms.

A Marxist Class Analysis of Academic Marxists

It is understandable that the idealist perspective appeals to academic intellectuals even if their term for utopian idealism is "historical materialism." If reality is constituted by language, one can change it at the word processor. Indeed, there are remarkable similarities between the characteristic ideas of Theory and those of the prerevolution Russian radical intelligentsia whose ideas did change the world. Perhaps a way of explaining such an odd conjunction across time and space is to bring to bear Marx's transnational conception of class. The thesis has been advanced, most persuasively by Alvin Gouldner, that those who primarily work with words applied not to matter but to other words form a *New Class* and that this privileging of language is obviously idealist: "Such a standpoint . . . is exactly what Marx had denounced as idealism, i.e., philosophical idealism, *the accounting of ideas in terms of other ideas*" (195). Indeed, Marx attacked the Young Hegelians for merely "fighting against '*phrases*.' They forget, however, that to these phrases they themselves are only opposing other phrases, and that they are in no way combating the real existing world when they are merely combating the phrases of this world" (*German Ideology*, 41). The phrase-mongering New Class is a social formation that Theory has not "interrogated."

One can, in fact, explain the academic intellectual class's attraction to Marxist socialism in Marxist terms. The anarchist leader Michael Bakunin predicted that Marx's version of socialism would lead not to liberation but to the domination of the New Class, and a Polish anarchist "depicted socialism as an ideology formulated in the interest of the intelligentsia, 'an emergent privileged class,' whose capital consists of higher education. In a socialist state they would achieve dominance by replacing the old class of capitalists as administrators and experts" (Pipes, *Russian Revolution*, 1991, 135). Once into power they put ideal economic theory into practice, thus wrecking the Russian economy, which even under the mismanagement of the tsars was the world's fifth largest (Pipes, *Bolshevik Regime*, 371).

Even Lenin finally *admitted* the economic failure, though blaming it on the Russian peasantry: "We had counted . . . on the [ability] of the proletarian state to organize by direct command state production and state distribution of goods in a Communist manner in a country of small peasants. Life has demonstrated our mistake" (quoted in Pipes, *Bolshevik Regime*, 397). But the mistake was in Lenin's Marxist idealist rationalism, the dream of a unified plan.

Thus what Philip Bryan Harper referred to as "the increasingly rationalized mode of production that characterizes industrial capitalism" was more true of Marxist socialism than capitalism. Harper seems to blame capitalism for what even Marx recognized as the inevitable results of large-scale industrialism. Marx himself declared, "All combined labour on a grand scale requires, more or less, a directing authority, in order to secure the harmonious working of the individual activities, and to perform the general functions that have their origin in the action of the combined organism, as distinguished from the action of its separate organs" (*Capital*, 363).

In fact, what Marx detested was not economic rationalism but economic *ir*rationalism, mankind's dependence on circumstance and chance, as in the variations of supply and demand central to a market economy. This conception underlies Marx's claim, in *The German Ideology*, that bourgeois freedom is illusory: "In imagination individuals seem freer under the domination of the bourgeoisie than before, because their conditions of life seem accidental; in reality, of course, they are less free, because they are more subject to the violence of things" (84). In *Capital*, he notes that "chance and caprice have full play in distributing . . . producers and their means of production among the various branches of industry" (390). However, "*All-round* dependence . . . will be transformed by . . . Communist revolution into the control and conscious mastery of these powers, which, born of the action of men on one another, have till now overawed and governed men as powers completely alien to them" (*German Ideology*, 55). Obviously the embodiment of such a vision requires a rationalized "control and mastery" on a grand scale. Alexandre Kojeve noted the problem with applied intellectualist idealism: "The real is that which *resists*. One is completely wrong to think that the real resists thought. . . . The Real resists Action, and not thought" (quoted in Dews, 255). Theory does not seem to work very well when it bumps up against a reality that ultimately does not allow for reduction to pure sign. Bruno Latour has an apposite metaphor: "What do you call those things that make a car slow down? A speed bump. The British call it the 'sleeping policeman.' I like to say, 'the sleeping policeman is not a sign. The sleeping policeman will break your damn car'" (Berreby, 24).

For that matter, some major Western Marxist theoreticians seem uncertain as to how their cars run. Douglas Johnson, a British admirer of a French Marxist theoretician highly influential on American literary criticism, Louis Althusser, indulgently notes, "His superb intellectual analysis was in contrast to his naiveté. He only just [at the time Johnson met him] seemed to have discovered that a shift system existed in French factories" (Althusser, *The Future,* xiv). Althusser has been given credit for de-Stalinizing Marxism (Benton, xi), but this may come down to his removing it from any relation to reality. For instance, Althusser proclaims that "the only possible definition of communism—if one day it were to exist in the world—*is the absence of any relationships based on the market,* that is to say of exploitative class relations and the domination of the state" (*The Future,* 225).

This is orthodox enough; at the center of Marx's thought was his desire to abolish the market. But what Althusser would substitute for the market is not clear. He appears to be a Cargo Cult economist. Moreover, he takes for granted, in hegemonic fashion, the equation of the Market to exploitation and especially state domination. But *without* a market and the essential information of what people want and how much they want it, the only way the economy *can* function is by a command economy, which itself necessitates totalitarian state domination. In this respect, the progression from Marx to Lenin to Stalin was not a historical accident but a predictable relation of Marxist ideology to communist practice.

This was strongly argued by F. A. Hayek, but even for those who would dismiss his case as "Western logic" there is the evidence of history. One of the *actual* economic innovations of communism was the divestment from workers of what Marx and Althusser saw as the false bourgeois appearance of freedom to choose and change occupations. As Kolakowski points out, "Once the market is abolished there is no longer any free sale of labour or competition between workers, and police coercion is therefore the only means of allocating 'human resources'" (3:29).

Marxist socialism even restored a form of oppression the tsars had given up by not only requiring internal passports for travel in the USSR but forbidding them to peasants, thus effectually reestablishing serfdom (Kolakowski, 3:29). China introduced internal passports in 1956 (Becker, 52). [It is only fair to say that the USSR eventually restored peasants their passports in the 1970s (Kolakowski, 3:39).] Althusser claimed that his version of Marxism "casts light on that subtle everyday domination beneath which can be glimpsed, in the forms of political democracy, for example, what Lenin, following Marx, called the dictatorship of the bourgeoisie" (*Lenin,* 133). The Marxist form of domination cannot be accused of subtlety.

For Althusser and Western Marxism, economics is an afterthought. Occasionally some of Marx's economic concepts such as surplus value, use value, and exchange value are flourished but without discernible real content, which is not surprising given their obsolescence in contemporary economics. Indeed, Althusser's influence was based on his moving Marxist theory away from economics, with its uncongenial susceptibility to empirical evidence, onto the safer ground of ideology. Here is where some of Marx's thinking still has some purchase. Marx had an undeniable brilliance as an analyst as well as producer of ideology. Perhaps we should think of the Marx who still has relevance as not an economist or a philosopher but a rhetorician. This may explain the elective affinity of Marxism and English departments.

Alienation and Ideology

The key terms in Marx's analysis of capitalist ideology and his production of what became New Class ideology are "alienation" and "ideology." Alienation explains what is wrong with capitalism, and ideology explains how it hides what is wrong through the production of modes of false consciousness. Moreover, alienation already *is* ideology. Alienation is the necessary condition for the production of those modes of false consciousness that constitute the hegemony of the capitalist social formation.

"Alienation" was a term borrowed by Marx from philosophical discourse, which drew it from religious discourse. It is a central concept in Hegel, but though Marx knew it from Hegel, his use of it was more influenced by Ludwig Feuerbach. In the simplest formulation, it is the feeling of being estranged from oneself and one's world. Feuerbach's crucial move, a reductive version of Hegel's more complex idea, was to turn alienation from an expression of religious sensibility to a critique of religious illusion. Alienation was not metaphysical and profound but historical and remediable. The Christian religion for Feuerbach is no more than "the relation of man to himself, or more correctly to his own nature (i.e., his subjective nature); but a relation to it, viewed as a nature apart from his own. . . . All the attributes of the divine nature are, therefore, attributes of the human nature" (14). God's superiority consists solely of our own projected qualities: "To enrich God, man must become poor; that God may be all, man must be nothing" (26). In sum, "religion alienates our own nature from us and represents it as not ours" (236). All we need to end alienation is a repo job on God.

Marx virtually paraphrases Feuerbach in the opening passage of *The German Ideology*:

> Hitherto men have constantly made up for themselves false conceptions about themselves, about what they are and what they ought to be. They have arranged their relationships according to their ideas of God, of normal man, etc. The phantoms of their brains have got out of their hands. They, the creators, have bowed down before their creations. Let us liberate them from the chimeras, the ideas, dogmas, imaginary beings under the yoke of which they have pined away. Let us revolt against the rule of thoughts. (37)

This formulation became the most fruitful legacy of Western Marxism: Man is alienated and oppressed because he mistakes the human for the divine and the historical for the natural. False consciousness, then, is the lack of recognition that what oppresses one is not external and objective but a kind of frozen human thought.

Marx's analysis of how exploitation is masked by pretending that cultural choices are natural forces is the basis of what is called cultural studies or cultural critique and is central to New Historicism and Theory generally, allowing Theory to do what it does best: analyze rhetoric, oppose phrases to other phrases. Slight modifications of Marx's basic concept of ideology such as those in Foucault's discursive systems and epistemes, Gramsci's hegemony, and Althusser's ideological state apparatuses all come down to attempts to pin the ideological tail on the "bourgeois" donkey.

Besides allowing Theory to play on its home field of rhetoric, alienation and ideology explained something very mysterious: why so few people have enlisted in the effort to bring about the socialist paradise, the obvious advantages of which have been outlined above. This is why ideology has become the fetishized commodity of the academic thinking classes.

Civil Society and Its Enemies

An explanation of what Theory sees as a remarkably retrograde choice is possible not only by restoring the actual performance of communism as the mysterious missing comparison but by a less hegemonically prescribed look at how capitalism, the market, and Western democracy work. Only the most orthodox free marketers dispute that a considerable amount of unfairness, irrationality, and social harm is historically apparent in the workings of capitalism. Some of these are remediable, as in legislation that forbade the exploitation of children in factory labor, shortened working hours, legalized unions, environmental regulation, and so on. Yet it seems that a certain degree of unfairness and irrationality is intrinsic, built into the system. It is arguable, however, that this very irrationality may enable a cultural and ethical as well as economic performance that, flawed as it undoubtedly is, still works notably better than that of actually existing Marxist socialism.

Peter L. Berger's formulation is instructive:

> By comparison with socialism, capitalism is uncontrolled, turbulent, "messy."
> This quality has an intrinsic affinity with spontaneous institutions of partici-
> pation. Such institutions, however, function as "schools for democracy." The
> individual who has learned to participate in decision making on the level of
> a village council or a farmers' association learns the skills that will eventually
> pay off in the formal processes of democratic politics. (85)

Berger here focuses on the crucial role of what Hegel and others called "civil society," the ensemble of organizations and activities that are to some degree outside the state sector. This includes the market but also much more:

Most of these institutions have little to do with capitalism or even with economic interests of any kind. However, for the same reasons that capitalism is
inimical to totalitarianism, capitalism favors mediating structures. It "leaves
room" for them, precisely because it creates a highly dynamic zone that
is relatively autonomous vis-à-vis the state. By contrast, socialist societies
are much more prone to try to control, or to integrate politically, all these
groupings which, by their very existence, threaten the overall rational design
of a "command economy." (85)

In this respect socialist societies take their cue directly from Marx.

Indeed, a main purpose of Marx's analysis of ideology is to delegitimize and
eventually destroy civil society. Civil society is not universal or ideal enough for
Marx: "The standpoint of the old materialism is civil society; the standpoint of
the new is human society, or social humanity" (*German Ideology*, 123). Civil society,
for Marx, *is* the alienated world: "In the *political community* he regards himself as
a *communal being;* but in *civil society* he is active as a *private individual*, treats other
men as means, reduces himself to a means, and becomes the plaything of alien
powers" (*Writings*, 225). Even religion comes under "the sphere of egoism, of the
bellum omnium contra omnes. It is no longer the essence of *community* but the essence
of *division*. It is now only the abstract confession of particular peculiarity, of *private
whim*, of caprice" (227). Freedom of conscience and the rights of man encoded
into French revolutionary declarations and various American state constitutions
are "only the rights of egoistic man, man separated from other men and from the
community" (235). The communist utopia would liberate the community and turn
division into wholeness.

These ideas became a recipe for disaster. The state predictably filled the vac-
uum of the pluralistic civil institutions Marxist socialism destroyed, and the result
was precisely the opposite of what Marx, with his mysteriously spontaneously
organized "society" and his undefined notion of "community," had envisioned. In
actual, as opposed to ideal, communism, the strongest "communities" were those
of the army and the police, the latter aided by a nationwide web of informers. The
relative success of the communist destruction of the "bourgeois" concept of individual integrity led not to ideal community but to an atomistic and opportunistic
ethos of all against all, a world best envisioned not by Marx but by Hobbes.

Cargo Cult Economics

The result of the Marxist experiment with a totalitarian state apparatus would
hardly have astonished Edmund Burke or James Madison, with their understanding
of the need for a relatively free play of various historically developed institutions.

But the leading British Marxist literary theorist, Terry Eagleton, and the leading American Marxist literary theorist, Frederic Jameson, seem not fully to realize this. Eagleton recognizes, in *The Illusions of Postmodernism*, that states founded on Marxist principles have not done well either economically or morally. But it is a mistake to infer anything from this since poor states, lacking the benefit of such factors as "developed productive forces," "a vigorous liberal-democratic tradition," and "a civil society in good working order" cannot *afford* Marxism (106). "Radical democracy," as Eagleton renames Marxism, will have something to redistribute in Western capitalist states. A fine insight, though, in his enthusiasm for a democratic Marxist civil society, he evidently fails to recall Marx's intense hostility to liberal democracy and civil society, and does not seem to notice that capitalism had everything to do with the development of the productive forces he believes will empower a Marxist world. But in the event that some rich state did try to afford Marxism, would it not have to revert to capitalism after its wealth was properly appropriated without new wealth being generated? A whole new meaning for business cycles!

To eyes unilluminated by Theory, radical democracy as the true meaning of socialism is one idealist abstraction tautologically defined as another idealist abstraction, and to call the result *materialism* seems odd.

If Eagleton has very nearly abandoned ship, Jameson generally keeps the faith. In *The Political Unconscious* he manages to dispose of the market economy in a subordinate clause: "The affirmation of radical feminism . . . that to annul the patriarchal is the most *radical* political act—insofar as it includes and subsumes more partial demands, such as the liberation of the commodity form, is , . . perfectly consistent with an expanded Marxian framework" (100). Since the commodity form is simply the form anything takes in being exchanged, Jameson is "orthodoxly" Marxist in opposing markets as such, yet he feels no need to explain the disastrous performance of command economies. In *Postmodernism, or, The Cultural Logic of Late Capitalism* he praises Bob Perelman's poem, "China," because "it does seem to capture something of the excitement of the New China—unparalleled in world history—the unexpected emergence between two superpowers of 'number three,' the freshness of a whole new object world produced by human beings in some new control over their collective destiny; the signal event, above all, of a collectivity which has become a new 'subject of history' and which, after the long subjection of feudalism and imperialism, again, speaks in its own voice, for itself, as though for the first time" (29).

The very concept of a country's "own voice" seems odd coming from a foe of capitalist reification, but there is a greater problem. It is doubtful that this voice could properly represent anyone who survived, much less perished in, the massive, administratively caused Chinese famine of 1958 to 1962, though this was a "signal event" of the "new China." Jasper Becker cites an American scholar's estimate that

30 million people died in the famine, noting that *Chinese* estimates were more in the 40 million range and that "several sources said that even larger figures of 50 to 60 million deaths were cited at internal meetings of senior party officials" (270–73).

It seems more accurate to narrow the voice of the new China down a bit— to that of Chairman Mao. "Since 1949 China had become a closed and tightly controlled state in which the Party wielded an absolute control over information" (Becker, 287). And Mao tightly controlled the Party. Thus who else *could* speak for the new China? Fortunately, we now have the portrayal of Mao by his personal physician: "In Li Zhisui's *The Private Life of Chairman Mao*, we are shown the human Mao, the chronic insomniac, who spent days on end in his nightclothes either in bed or beside his private swimming pool, impetuous, alternately depressed and animated, the freest man in China yet fond of rebellion, refusing to brush his teeth, dependent on barbiturates and sexually insatiable" (cited in Link, "Someone Else," 8). Another hero of the left, Fidel Castro, is described by G. Cabrera Infante as "the only free man in Cuba" (cited in Gallagher, 7). Theory's recommended voices of liberation from our commoditized world are less than reassuring.

Of course, under capitalism self-interest can operate in quite harmful ways. The founding fathers of the United States were so aware of the power of self-interest that they built checks and balances of competing class interests into the fabric of the Constitution, proving more politically sophisticated than Marx, who believed that under communism self-interest, like the state, would magically wither away. Or than Lenin, Stalin, and Mao, who believed that if they eliminated the retrograde, the remnant would be purified. (Greta Garbo as the commissar in *Ninotchka* memorably responds to a question about the purges with "There will be fewer but better Russians.")

Really Existing Economic Systems

Leaving comparative performances aside for a moment, it seems open to question that buying and selling are intrinsically degrading. This is generally an unexamined progressive assumption though progressives can invoke Marx, for whom a market economy produced the "haggling, mean and niggardly spirit which still clung to all merchants and to the whole mode of carrying on trade" (*German Ideology*, 77). This elitist, essentially aristocratic view of trade ignores the fashion in which the market economy has extraordinarily widened possibilities of personal choice, self-fashioning. The protean self, so admired by postmodernists, needed the anonymity of large cities, the commercially enabled choice of lifestyles to move in and out of, to combine and refigure in new packagings of expressive styles derived from various cultures and subcultures.

A delightful example of the multicultural possibilities of commerce is the observation of the intrepid Victorian explorer, Mary Kingsley: "When you first appear among people who have never seen anything like you before, they naturally regard you as a devil; but when you want to buy or sell with them, they recognize there is something human and reasonable about you" (quoted by Langer, 28). At the very least, actual historical evidence as well as comparisons with alternative systems (and not merely ideals of them) ought to be considered before accepting Theory's unargued dogma of the evil of the market economy.

Particular accusations against capitalism, such as that it is the primary cause of subordination of women, prejudice against gays and lesbians and depredations against the ecology, though taken for granted by Theory, do not hold up well against the return of the repressed comparison. Thus "feminists have often been less hasty than Marxists to condemn all facets of capitalism, arguing that the experience of urban culture and even of consumerism has allowed women to experience new freedoms and pleasures denied them by traditional patriarchal constraints" (Felski, "Feminism," 50). In contrast, in contemporary Communist China, "the cultural preference for boys and China's ruthlessly enforced child-bearing restrictions have resulted in the wholesale destruction of girl babies through gross neglect, abandonment, infanticide and, in recent years, the targeted abortion of female babies" (Herbert, A23).

Gays and lesbians have indeed suffered from vicious persecution in Western, democratic, capitalist America. Yet it was this "social formation" that enabled their emergence, once sexuality became more re-creative than procreative. John D'Emilio notes that in capitalist urban space:

> Ideologically, heterosexual expression came to be a means of establishing intimacy, promoting happiness, and experiencing pleasure. In divesting the household of its economic independence and fostering the separation of sexuality from procreation, capitalism has created conditions that allow some men and women to organize a personal life around their erotic/emotional attraction to their own sex. It has made possible the formation of urban communities of lesbians and gay men and, more recently, of a politics based on sexual identity. (D'Emilio, 104)

The looseness of American consumerist identity has proved helpful for sexual minorities, certainly under threat in America but far less so than in more communal societies such as Marxist Cuba, which quarantines those with AIDS, and Iran, where one of Foucault's heroes, the Ayatollah Khomeini, ordered the execution of homosexuals.

That some American corporations have despoiled the environment is true. Jameson blames "capitalism": "Ecological damage is a subtext of capitalist fungibility in general: the technological transformation of all forms of ground and raw material, including space itself, into the indifferent materials of commodification and the purely formal occasions for profit" (*Seeds of Time*, 165). But is ecological damage primarily the result of capitalism or industrialism? Environmental regulation has had some notable successes in capitalist America, as in the cleanup and revitalization of the Hudson River. Doubtless some American industries wish they had the carte blanche enjoyed by industry in the USSR with its "awesome devastation wreaked on the flat, open landscape by more than seventy years of unchecked industrial and residential development. The furious technological 'progress' promoted in the name of the bright collective future of Communism has left behind an ugly legacy of pollution, deforestation and depopulation" (Robinson, 14). In the "new China" praised by Jameson, there is massive pollution and depletion of farmland (Link, Review of Vaclav Smil). The *New York Times* details ecological disasters in Badui, China (Kristof, 1), and Muynak, Uzbekistan (Kinzer, 4).

The Marxist Jeremiad

My emphasis has been on the silent assumptions of Theory and how they stand up to comparison. I now turn to the most interesting application of ideology theory to American literature, the work of Sacvan Bercovitch, an undoubtedly authoritative figure not only as a professor at Harvard but as general editor of a new literary history of the United States. Bercovitch's innovation was to demonstrate how American literature could be accused wholesale, thus allowing as extensive a retail market in applications of the doctrine as there are American texts. He universalizes ideological faultfinding in a fashion parallel to the tautologies of deconstruction, his method becoming a grid through which any text can be run. Drawing on Gramsci, Althusser, and others, Bercovitch demonstrates that all canonical American texts merely reflect, rather than transcend, oppressive capitalist American ideology. Even works that appear dissenting are always already co-opted by the dominant culture since they protest *in terms of* the American utopian dream. Bercovitch traces the inception of this ideological trap to John Winthrop's sermon on the Arbella, "A Modell of Christian Charity," which envisions the new colony as "a Citty upon a Hill," to be inhabited by a new chosen people who would be watched by all Christians hopeful of finding the right way. With such a divinely ordained responsibility, the Puritans would be deserving of especially harsh punishment from God for any faltering on the path. Thus the Puritan Jeremiads that attacked Puritans for backsliding were evidence not of the collapse of this belief in Puritan (and later American) exceptionalism but a reaffirmation of it. So, from then on, whenever an American writer attacked dominant American values, he or she was *really* defending them.

Bercovitch's formulation usefully reverses that aspect of American studies that Michael Denning accuses of complicity with the Cold War and American capitalism: "For this American Studies, 'American marxism' was surely an oxymoron; Americanism substituted for marxism as an antidote" (358). Denning's title, " 'The Special American Conditions': Marxism and American Studies," comes from the attempts of Marx and Engels to explain the failure of socialism to become a major factor in America. Bercovitch's formulation allows every American book to be read primarily *as this explanation:* Marxism can substitute for Americanism as an antidote. It is true that Bercovitch belatedly cautions his disciples against too vulgar an application: "We come to feel, in reading these works, that the American ideology is a system of ideas in the service of evil rather than (like any ideology) a system of ideas wedded for good and evil to a social order" ("Problem of Ideology," 638). Bercovitch goes on "to add, as emphatically as possible, that the argument I have just outlined does not in any sense diminish the aesthetic power of the texts themselves. It does not even require, on the critic's part, an adversary response toward the culture" (646).

I do not doubt Bercovitch's sincerity, but reading the work influenced by him and even his own work hardly bears out these assertions. Indeed, much of this work, with its blindness to apt comparison, is a *version* of the American Jeremiad: "The apocalyptic view of history tends, unrealistically, to categorize nations and actions as wholly bad or wholly good; this fact has encouraged Americans to judge history of even this nation by the same standard" (Tuveson, 132). Much of Theory uses the Marxian-Althusserian-Gramscian-Bercovitchian method to portray America as the Great Satan.

This is not to deny that Bercovitch is on to something. The concept of American exceptionalism has been pushed way beyond bounds, both in affirmation and denunciation. Jack P. Greene's *The Intellectual Construction of America* and Seymour Martin Lipset in *Continental Divide* argue a far more modest and carefully comparative case for a degree of American exceptionalism. (Lipset's comparison, in fact, is with Bercovitch's own native land of Canada.) What Bercovitch really addresses is the same exception that bothers Denning, the failure of Marxist socialism to become as viable an alternative as it did in Italy, where it was the dominant opposition for many years after World War II, or, say, in Poland, where it was put in power by the Russian army. The underlying idea is clear when Bercovitch declares, "To define injustice through particular violations of free enterprise (or its constituent elements, such as social mobility, open opportunity, and self-fulfillment) is to consecrate free enterprise as *the* just society" ("Problem of Ideology," 644). It is clear that Bercovitch means the *whole system* here and precisely distinguishes a desirable repudiation of this system from mere piecemeal reforms. But what other *whole system* than Marxist socialism could he have in mind? Yet Bercovitch never stoops to specific comparisons, thus leaving the alternative in the realm of the ideal.

Not only does Bercovitch avoid specific comparisons between America and other cultural systems that he seems to call for but also differences within America, thus nullifying American diversity. He restores the New England cultural hegemony that had been embodied in Barrett Wendell's genteel and provincial "history" of "American" literature, one that those outside New England satirically called "The Literary History of Harvard College." The materialistic, non-apocalyptic colonial South is terra incognita in Bercovitch's mapping of American discourse. Typically few of Bercovitch's acolytes are even aware of Jack P. Greene's challenge to Bercovitch's thesis of *The Puritan Origins of the American Self.* In *Pursuits of Happiness,* Greene argues the alternative Chesapeake Bay vision of the American self: "Important though it has sometimes been the concept of 'national election' seems never to have been so pervasively and persistently influential in shaping American culture as the notion of America as a place peculiarly favorable for the quest for the good life, defined as the pursuit of individual happiness and material achievement" (205).

This chapter has described the rarely examined hegemonical structure of ideological assumptions of the Marxist branch of Theory. As in hegemonical constructions generally, these assumptions are taken as axiomatic grounds of argument, not themselves in need of argument or evidence. The use of literature in Theory is to teach a political orthodoxy that does not fare well when argued in specific, comparative *political* terms. Indeed, transforming literary criticism into the study of literature as "Ideological State Apparatus" was the perfect solution for academics who had little grasp of real world economic and political dilemmas: " 'Theoretical practice' in the academic arena was thus the site of ideological battle. . . . Scholars in their seminars were on the front line, and need feel guilty no more" (Tony Judt, cited in Seaton, 254). In succeeding chapters I examine how Theory furthered the Marxist narrative first by evolving new heroines and heroes to replace the disappointing proletariat and then by combining with poststructuralism to further evade the problems presented by history and reality.

But I wish in conclusion to emphasize that my purpose in this chapter is in no way to affirm a totally unrestrained and unregulated capitalist order, the devil take the hindmost. The distressing aspect of Theory is, once again, how it confirms Gresham's Law in the realm of liberal and even radical political discourse, its bad political thinking driving out good. American radical politics is crippled not by the downfall of Marxist socialist ideology but by its academic hegemony. Marxist utopianism, with its inherent tendency toward totalitarianism, dominates radical intellectual discourse, displacing productive political thinking. Vaunting itself as a liberating discourse, the Theory notion of ideology is flagrantly elitist and antidemocratic.

Those unfamiliar with the current academic situation may think this an overstatement. But it is *overtly* proclaimed by such influential progressives as Paula Rothenberg: "The protection of property rights and the maintenance of patriarchal privilege will not yield without a struggle, and it will be the job of socialism to see to it that these interests are suppressed and eliminated even when and if this runs counter to the expressed will of the people and their commitment to the very civil liberties that liberal democracy has taught them elevate above all substantive matters" (49). Rothenberg is in perfect accord with Marx.

3

Visible Saints: The Politics of Standpoint Epistemology

Standpoint Epistemology

The combination of Marxism and deconstruction, each discourse reinforcing the other's ideological self-privilegings, became hegemonic in American English departments at the very time their contradictions were leading to their obsolescence in their sites of origin—France and the Eastern bloc. But an essential ingredient was lacking. The center of Marxist dramatic pathos had been the proletariat, long gone missing. Additionally the terms "American" and "proletariat" had never convincingly gone together. The new narrative needed a new protagonist to embody the received word, the "progressive" logos. In Alvin Gouldner's phrase, Theory went "shopping for an agent" (Gouldner, 26).

Theory found its hero in women and minorities, conceived in the same fashion as the proletariat had been. This maneuver is known in feminist theory as standpoint epistemology. The feminist theorist Sandra Harding describes the Marxist belief that "the proletariat, guided by Marxist theory and by class struggle, became the ideal knowers, the group capable of using observation and reason to grasp the true form of social relations, including our relations with nature. This Marxist successor to bourgeois science was . . . to provide one social group—the proletariat—with the knowledge and power to lead the rest of the species toward emancipation" ("Instability," 654). As Harding notes, the "standpoint tendency in feminist epistemology . . . seeks to substitute women or feminists (the accounts differ) for the proletariat as the potentially ideal agents of knowledge." In contrast, "men's characteristic social experience, like that of the bourgeoisie, hides from them the politically imposed nature of the social relations they see as natural" (655).

Harding, deploying standpoint epistemology, is celebrated for declaring that because of Newton's metaphors for science achieving mastery over nature his

Principia should be renamed "Newton's Rape Manual" (*Science Question*, 113). Nevertheless, she had reservations about how far the concept could go without its essentializing Woman as a single, transhistorical Knower. Nancy Hartsock, in her highly influential essay, "The Feminist Standpoint," takes it the whole route. The position of proletarians and women is similar: "Women and workers inhabit a world in which the emphasis is on change rather than stasis, a world characterized by interaction with natural substances rather than separation from nature, a world in which quality is more important than quantity, a world in which the unification of mind and body is inherent in the activities performed" (222–23). Both have a superior standpoint but women are *more* superior: "The feminist standpoint . . . is related to the proletarian standpoint, but deeper going" (222). For instance, "The female experience in reproduction represents a unity with nature which goes beyond the proletarian experience of interchange with nature" (225).

Hartsock assumes rather than argues these proletarian/bourgeois, female/male oppositions and seems not to have considered, for one, that the most debilitating aspect of factory labor was its deadly repetition, its stasis. Indeed, there are good arguments for reversing all her oppositions and some evident contradictions in others. One such contradiction comes when she agrees with Women Against Violence Against Women that " 'the normal male is sexually aggressive in a brutal and demeaning way' " (230) and proceeds to valorize women throughout her essay for being oppositional to violence. Whether or not this sweeping opposition is valid, it is in contradiction with her swerve back to Marx for a final solution to the problem of social transformation that combines "socialist revolution" with gender revolution (233). Hartsock has a to-do list for socialist revolution: "The abolition of the division between mental and manual labor cannot take place simply by means of adopting worker self-management techniques, but instead requires the abolition of private property, the seizure of state power, and lengthy post-revolutionary class struggle" (233). Transforming gender relations that have been unequal since the beginning of recorded history would require measures at least equally strenuous. What Hartsock does not explain is that if women, because of their superior standpoint, are going to be the vanguard of this dual revolution, and if a major aspect of women's superiority is their rejection of male violence, then who is going to do the killing? Especially during "the lengthy post-revolutionary class struggle," which is, as Hartsock apparently recognizes, when most of the killing—of the politically incorrect—was done in Russia and Cambodia? This point is all the more problematic in that, as I argued in chapter 2, it is not clear that all this killing really liberated anyone. If, on the other hand, Hartsock does not have a violent revolution in mind, she should explain what other kind of Marxist revolution there is.

There are other problems with standpoint epistemology at least in its stronger versions. An obvious one is that standpoint epistemology seems, *in principle*, less designed to promote equity than to enunciate a new elite, though perhaps one confined to university English departments. A notable development in feminist discourse has been the use of the standpoint phrase, "As a woman, I . . ." It seems to me a problem that the phrase presents no sense of limitation; it is rarely used except as an admission of perfection. Is there anything that a feminist *cannot* see from her standpoint? But to say, "As a man, I . . ." could function in Theory only as an admission of epistemological deficit. Terry Caesar sums it up: "So what is a man? Ultimately an object for feminist discourse. Insofar as he can't represent himself in his own voice . . . [he] is curiously like what a woman is in prefeminist discourse" (11). Turnabout may well be fair play or the best revenge or both but hardly the cosmic equity that feminists claim to strive for.

The most elaborate argument for standpoint epistemology is Ellen Messer-Davidow's essay, "The Philosophical Bases of Feminist Literary Criticism." The essay centered a *New Literary History* issue on "Feminist Directions," was followed by nine responses and Messer-Davidow's response to the responses, and has been reprinted in other feminist anthologies. Here, if anywhere, should be a representative presentation of the feminist standpoint in literary studies. But what the essay clearly calls for is the substitution of feminist politics for literary studies: "The subject of feminist literary criticisms appears to be not literature but the feminist study of ideas about sex and gender that people express in literary and critical media" (77). In contrast to traditional critics' objectivist claims, "feminist critics stand forth in a domain of our own making, revealing our perspectivity—and theirs" (88). This briefly sounds conducive to a dialogue between the perspectivities but it becomes apparent that the feminist perspective is morally superior: It explains the false consciousness of the traditional perspective through the feminist perspective in which "'Truth' no longer functions in the traditional senses of gauging the universality and predictability of knowledge, nor does 'verisimilitude' demand accuracy in representing 'reality.' Instead equity and epistemic awareness are the standards for self-conscious, other-conscious relational ways of knowing" (89).

The argument is circular: Feminists have their awareness as a standard for verifying their awareness. Messer-Davidow and Joan Hartman's "Introduction: A Position Statement" in *(En)gendering Knowledge* is even more overtly tautological: "While humanists 'find' value in artifacts and scientists 'find' it in facts, feminist knowers . . . affirm the value of our own values in the production of knowledge" (3). This seems to mean that feminists do not need to discover what they always already know. When Messer-Davidow declares we must "delineate all the elements . . . men have used in constructing their reality and show it for the artifact it is" (74), she ignores the problem that the feminist standpoint is also an artifact.

Here, as elsewhere, the strategy of Theory is to formulate general prescriptive rules of discourse that are binding on their opposition but not on themselves. Thus Messer-Davidow confidently asserts that "a woman who accepts the traditional view of woman as other is self-alienated. Feminists must not embrace the self/other dichotomy in claiming our selfhoods, but develop a perspectivity that confers selfhood all around" ("Philosophical Bases," 82). This seems directed at French feminism, and Messer-Davidow could be "right." But again her argument is that these women are deluded by a "false" epistemology rather than that they have an alternative perspective. Quite a few beings seem left out of the selfhood that Messer-Davidow's perspectivity entitles *her* to "confer." An obvious problem with Messer-Davidow's perspective is that while she puts "truth," "verisimilitude," "fact," and "find" in scare quotes as epistemologically suspect terms used to promote self-interested positions, she uses *equity,* the practical meaning of which is one of the most disputed concepts in philosophy, as if it were self-evident.

In sum, Messer-Davidow's feminist standpoint values are grounded in tautology and self-privileging. Nor can she discover anything new, whether about women or anything else, that she does not presume to already know. Literary works are conceived not as personal and cultural creations one can learn from but as blank surfaces on which to project always already known values. Messer-Davidow scants aesthetic concerns:

> As literary critics we want to affirm, as Wayne Booth declares, that "art works exist as valued achievements of a high order." On the other hand, as feminist critics we want to affirm that the equitable disposition of people is a valued achievement of a high order. The tension surfaces agonizingly when these two allegiances clash and we are forced to pass judgment, say, on Milton's great epic. But great in what sense? If we weren't thinking about gender while thinking about literature, we wouldn't be torn between the excellent crafting of a work and the pernicious effects of its ideology. ("Philosophical Bases," 72)

But Booth is misrepresented as being on the opposite side of this rather crude split between literary formalism and ideological content because it is a split he does not make. His interest is in "The Ethics of Fiction" (the subtitle of *The Company We Keep*). True, in contrast to Messer-Davidow, he does not believe that these ethics are transparent but that they must be interpreted out of a work's complexity of style. For Messer-Davidow, it seems more a matter of appliqué criticism: slap on the label of progressive or reactionary with no tensions, ambiguities, or indirections allowed.

Messer-Davidow's ideas are not only inadequate but coercive. The coercive aspect of standpoint is front and center in Dale M. Bauer's *College English* essay, "The Other 'F' Word: The Feminist in the Classroom." This essay draws from Bauer's adaptation to feminism of Bakhtin's idea of the dialogic novel in *Feminist Dialogics,* the introduction to which is excerpted in Warhol and Herndl's influential anthology *Feminisms*. Here, Bauer posits that "we acquire 'ourselves' by engaging in our dialogue with others, and especially with texts that challenge our own beliefs. In the act of reading, we divest ourselves of the illusion of monolithic selfhood" (676). If this is what Bauer means by dialogism, the more of it the better. Unfortunately, it is not.

What Bauer really means by the dialogical is clearly expressed in her *College English* essay, "The Other 'F' Word: The Feminist in the Classroom," where it functions as a way of using "one kind of mastery, feminist and dialogic in practice, against another, monologic and authoritarian." There is not a dialogue between the feminist professor and retrograde student since the dialogic is already embodied in the professor's self-evidently true standpoint. Rather the professor practices "a kind of counter-indoctrination, a debriefing" of the ideology that has presumably been implanted in the student (387). Bauer's rhetorical strategy is two pronged: "to break down resistances and offer identifications" (389). The identification is provided by the preexistent goals of the feminist agenda: "The feminist agenda offers a goal towards our students' conversions to emancipatory critical action" (389).

The obvious question here is what happened to dialogue in the dialogic since the only model here presented is that between the politically correct feminist professor and the politically incorrect resistant student. Conversion requires stern measures: "In teaching identification and teaching feminism, I overcome a vehement insistence on pluralistic relativism or on individualism" ("The Other 'F' Word," 391); "my feminist pedagogy serves to break down their will to believe in pedagogy's neutral agenda" ("Bauer Responds," 103). It may be that the students' minds have been colonized by the dominant culture but, far from teaching students "how to resist" ("The Other 'F' Word," 391), Bauer intends to colonize their voice with *her* voice, the voice of orthodox academic progressive discourse. She says, "We ask them to recognize identity—and politics—as social constructions" (391) but does not so relativize feminist identity or feminist politics. Certainly her students are not invited to identify with the literary tricksters that Bakhtin so admired, figures who affirm, "the right to be 'other' in this world, the right not to make common cause with any single one of the existing categories that life makes available; none of these categories quite suits them, they see the underside and the falseness of every situation" (Bakhtin, 159). In sum, a more accurate term for Bauer's pedagogy might be feminist monologic.

Bauer's confidence in the correctness of her monologic is clearly one of the fruits of feminist standpoint epistemology. It is instructive to see how enabling her feminist standpoint proves on a work that exemplifies Bakhtin's "dialogic imagination," Edith Wharton's *Summer*.

Bauer is certainly true to her principles in her analysis of this novel. She declares that she draws out and discusses resistances to feminism "by compelling students to work through them in literature by confronting fears and values mediated by the form of fiction" ("The Other 'F' Word," 393). This accords with Messer-Davidow's program of teaching "not literature but the feminist study of ideas about sex and gender that people express in literary and critical media." Indeed, the problems with Messer-Davidow's theory are exemplified in Bauer's practice. Bauer's practice is opposite to what Deborah Kennedy calls for in her response to Bauer's *College English* essay: "I try to be a feminist teaching the subject . . . not a feminist using the subject as an excuse for programming students" (102). For Bauer, *Summer* is "a case study of the controversies within twentieth-century discourses of pregnancy and reproductive rights" (35). Thus when Charity Royall refuses the sexual attempt upon her of her guardian, a man old enough to be her father, instead being attracted to "handsome" (Wharton's epithet for him), young Lucius Harney, this becomes for Bauer how Wharton has her heroine "exemplify the independence and assertiveness of the new woman" (Bauer, *Brave New World*, 29). To my mind this ignores an ordinary adolescent response in favor of an abstract political positioning deriving from Bauer's own prescripted standpoint.

At another point, with the feminist conception of the homosocial clearly in mind, Bauer declares that Harney "gives in to his desire when Charity confesses Royall's attempted seduction, as if to suggest that the patriarch's acknowledgment of Charity as an object of someone else's sexual desire sanctions his own. . . . Charity Royall becomes a woman that a gentleman need not take any pains to respect" (*Brave New World*, 40). Charity explains Royall's motivation as his wanting the convenience of a prostitute in the home "'so's 't he wouldn't have to go out.'" Harney's response seems rather more complicated than Bauer indicated: "Harney stared at her. For a moment he did not seem to seize her meaning; then his face grew dark. 'The damned hound! The villainous low hound!' His wrath blazed up, crimsoning him to the temples. 'I never dreamed—good God, it's too vile,' he broke off, as if his thoughts recoiled from the discovery" (Wharton, 168). Far from cheery homosocial complicity, Harney is horrified and disgusted at Royall. He responds to Charity with a chivalrous, protective passion that segues into sexual arousal, a dubious progression that itself calls for feminist deconstruction but of a more subtle kind than that for which Bauer's preconceptions allow. Complicating the situation is that Wharton hints a complicity not between Harney and Royall but between Charity and Harney in this consummation of their mutual attraction. Though not the 1990s feminist Bauer wants her to be, Charity does have a certain unconventionality and independence, as well as being notably shrewd and manipulative when she wants to be. For instance, Charity is genuinely shocked and repulsed at Royall's failed seduction but also knows how to use it: "Nothing now would ever shake her rule in the red house" (38). I suggest she uses it again, perhaps not altogether consciously, with Harney. At any rate, Bauer, reading through ready-made interpretive schemes, bars herself from perceiving the complexity of Wharton's world.

In any terms, the relation between Charity and her guardian is disturbing. This disturbance is, however, stabilized by taking him, from a feminist reading standpoint, for a patriarchal villain. This despite Bauer's disagreement with Ammons's feminist standpoint on *Summer* as one that "forecloses any contradictions" (36) and is "too univocal" (35). Royall is the major patriarch of North Dormer, and his relation to Charity as guardian, would-be seducer, and, eventually, husband is emotionally incestuous. Moreover, while trying to hold Charity to the narrow prevailing code of female decorum he benefits from the double standard that allows him to occasionally indulge, as Bauer notes, in "drinking, debauching, carousing" (39). The double standard is most flagrantly dramatized when Charity is shocked to see him drunk and consorting with prostitutes while Royall is simultaneously shocked to see her with Harney, unchaperoned and hatless!

Wharton certainly points to male privilege in *Summer*, but Bauer gilds the lily in her reading of the boarding school incident: "When [Royall] fails to send her off to boarding school after his wife's death, Charity realizes he has been undone by 'the thought of losing her.' . . . Depressed and stultified himself, Royall seeks to control Charity's sexuality, as Wharton shows how disinterestedness can mask a repressed desire for control" (*Brave New World*, 44). An alert reading, however, shows Royall precisely overcoming his desire to keep Charity close, to control her. If some readers cannot see this, it may be because they identify with Charity, who, throughout most of the novel, cannot see it either. Here is the scene that Charity interprets as Royall's decision to keep her home:

> After Mrs. Royall's death there was some talk of sending her to a boarding-school. Miss Hatchard suggested it, and had a long conference with Mr. Royall, who, in pursuance of her plan, departed one day for Starkfield to visit the institution she recommended. He came back the next day with a black face; worse, Charity observed, than she had ever seen him; and by that time she had had some experience.
>
> When she asked him how soon she was going to start he answered shortly, 'You ain't going,' and shut himself up in the room he called his office; and the next day the lady who kept the school at Starkfield wrote that 'under the circumstances' she was afraid she could not make room just then for another pupil.
>
> Charity was disappointed but she understood. (Wharton, 24–25)

What the feminist standpoint fails to understand here is that the Starkfield school turned away Charity because of the circumstances of her birth, her illegitimacy. Royall, a rather decisive man as patriarchs tend to be, did not go all the way to

Starkfield just to change his mind at the last moment, and, had he done so, he would not have come back in such a foul mood. His anger is a response to the slight to Charity, one he chooses not to pass on to her. An additional clue is that Charity gets a second chance, one that obviously would have had to have Royall's approval, when Miss Hatchard offers her a school at Nettleton. Charity refuses, declaring, "'I guess Mr. Royall's too lonesome.'" Miss Hatchard's response to this clarifies that, in her offer, she is acting for, not against, Royall:

> Miss Hatchard blinked perplexedly behind her eye-glasses. Her long frail face was full of puzzled wrinkles, and she leant forward, resting her hands on the arms of her mahogany armchair, with the evident desire to say something that ought to be said.
> "The feeling does you credit, my dear." (Wharton, 26)

Miss Hatchard is perplexed by Charity's comment because she knows Royall's actual intentions; she then interprets Charity as wishing to stay with Royall rather than as being coerced by his patriarchal power. She is, however, disturbed at Charity staying alone with Royall for the same reason as most critics of the novel: the sexual possibilities. This is what she has a desire to say and finally does say.

This reading requires that one go behind Charity's point of view and exercise some historical imagination about attitudes toward illegitimacy that one might find in a New England boarding school of the teens, neither of which seem possible for Bauer's version of the feminist standpoint. Yet Charity herself later recognizes the limitation of her view of Royall when she realizes that "she had regarded him only in relation to herself, and had never speculated as to his own feelings" (Wharton, 110). She then compounds her misunderstanding. Royall warns her that she has been compromised by having been seen in Harney's room at night, and she responds by accusing him:

> "Then it was you who put the lie into their mouths.—Oh, how I've always hated you!" she cried.
> She had expected a retort in kind, and it startled her to hear her exclamation sounding on through silence.
> "Yes, I know," Mr. Royall said slowly. "But that ain't going to help us much now." (112)

That Charity could suppose that Royall would disgrace her to the community shows how little she understands the kind of man he is and the feelings he has for her. He is a deeply flawed patriarch but an honorable one within terms of the values he holds by.

Bauer compounds Charity's misreading by taking Royall's attempt to make Harney face up to what this historical value system would construct as Royall's responsibilities in terms of a feminist theoretical conception: "If he cannot seduce Charity himself, Royall wants to force Harney to marry her, thereby literally enforcing the law-of-the-father over her" (*Brave New World*, 46). This despite Wharton's construction of the scene as Royall's "pathetic abdication of all authority over her" (114). It seems evident that Bauer regards Charity and Royall only in relation to the preconceptions of the feminist standpoint. Royall becomes a straw figure of the patriarchy, Charity a flawless feminist superwoman, a disservice to both these fascinating, complex characters. Thus Bauer's description of Charity as wanting "to see her sexual relation as countercultural" (*Brave New World*, 49) is part of the processing of Charity, the teens, and Wharton's novel into the critical conventions of contemporary, orthodox feminist politics, a procedure evidently in accord with Messer-Davidow's version of the "philosophical bases of feminist criticism."

Orthodox feminist criticism sanctifies female characters and writings, and demonizes male characters and writing by way of binary oppositions that always already demonstrate the superior moral and political perception of all women over all men. But Susan Lanser, a strongly feminist critic who does not follow the party line, points out that such difference is a critical artifact:

> The two basic gestures of U.S. feminist criticism [are] "deconstructing dominant male patterns of thought and social practice" and "reconstructing female experience previously hidden or overlooked." . . . In designating gender as the foundation for two very different critical activities, feminist criticism has embraced contradictory theories of literature, proceeding as if men's writings were ideological sign systems and women's writings were representations of truth, reading men's or masculinist texts with resistance and women's or feminist texts with empathy. (422)

This double standard occurs in critical reading of documentary evidence as well, with any claim of female victimization endorsed without skeptical scrutiny while any claim of male fairness is instantly "deconstructed."

How much more diverse, differentiated, vital, disturbing, enlivening, threatening, resonant, depressing, unnerving, and, above all, unexpected, contingent but ultimately real a world we get from the nonorthodox critics, the creative writers, and the "old" historians. Why replace the discovery of self and world that literature enables only for the purpose of inscribing a prescriptive, increasingly dated political ideology upon it? Rather than the enabling curiosity of scholarship we have academics who already know from the gender or race of a given writer what the writer "really" means and how to evaluate that meaning. If one is less interested, less willing to pay attention to fiction and film as opposed to political recruitment, why not do the politics directly? The answer may be that this would too much bare the device, revealing embarrassing contradictions in the politics along the lines of those examined in the previous chapter.

Ascriptive Identity

All this is not to say that identity politics have no pull. They have the attraction as well as the inherent problems of essential identities ascribed to certain groups, as with the supposed superiority of aristocrats. Ascriptive identity politics has the disadvantage of running counter to long-standing American conceptions of democracy.

The defining American move toward democratization was to redefine identity as voluntary, chosen, and enacted rather than inherent, imposed, and ascriptive. Past social orders thrust "on the individual an ascribed identity . . . while a modern conception of freedom includes the requirement that identities be chosen rather than ascribed" (Gellner, 80). It may be a strength of our society that "individual commitment to contract not status seems to be a foundation of this social order" (Gellner, 78) and that "status in the American experience is not ascribed but achieved" (B. Berger, 525).

Ascriptive identity went with expected and enforced deference toward social superiors. The radicalism of the American Revolution consisted largely in the move away from an ascriptive class status accorded deference. The historian Gordon Wood observes: "Ordinary Americans came to believe that no one in a basic down-to-earth and day-in and day-out manner was really better than anyone else. That was equality as no other nation has ever quite had it" (234). This equality was hardly universal, since race and gender still functioned as ascriptive. However, Pauline Maier argues that "*principles . . . stated to support American political independence rebounded upon domestic practices and were appropriated to serve the causes of other people, including slaves, women and religious minorities*" (10; my emphasis). The revolution raised the question of the consistency of American values regarding slavery (Wood, 186–87) and women and the family (146–47, 183–84), beginning a process still under way.

Standpoint theory, however, does not derive rights from extending the general conception of freedom to those historically but illogically excluded but fetishizes certain privileged identities as ideal. In so doing it runs counter to the American tradition of privileging the accomplishments of individuals over their ascriptive group identity. Basing one's politics on ascriptive characteristics is unlikely to convince those outside the ideal group identities. The problem of arguments validated not by argument but as assertions of ideal identity is that whatever one arrives at is fixed and nonnegotiable; disagreement is taken not as difference over a possibility or position but as difference over difference, an attack on one's being: "Persons are to be judged not by what they do or they say but by what they *are*. What you are is what your racial or sexual identity dictates. Your identity becomes the sole ground of politics, the sole determinant of political good and evil. Those who disagree with my 'politics,' then, are the enemies of my identity" (Elshtain, 53). Another problem is that identity, so conceived, tends to be fissionable, thus problematic for a critical mass of influence, not to mention alliance. There are not just women but women of color and not just women of color but lesbian women of color and all presumably have somewhat different positions among Messer-Davidow's "perspectivities." Thus Robyn R. Warhol and Diane Price Herndl follow feminist fashion in their anthology, *Feminisms*, by identifying themselves as "white middle-class heterosexual American feminist academics in our early thirties (to cover a number of the categories feminist criticism has lately been emphasizing as significant to one's reading and speaking positions" (ix). But how well do such identity assortments add up to a coherent position? Do Warhol and Herndl speak as one and for all others who occupy the designated positions? Would differences between them (if any) be solely the result of yet other subject positions they occupy but not the result of being free-thinking individuals?

Nina Baym objects more to such proliferation of subject positions than their claims to automatic authenticity: "The number of qualifiers needed to hyphenate the material 'woman' as she exists in time, space, and culture is uncountable. . . . Hyphenated women are allegories" ("Agony of Feminism," 115). Elsewhere she acutely observes: "My point would not be that there are no differences; but that when you start with a theory of difference, you can't see anything but" ("The Madwoman," 159). The problem, after all, with the illusoriness of identity is that it goes all the way up as well as all the way down. In disposing of integral selves Theory substitutes an infinity of subject positions each of which is as predetermined and monolithic as Theory supposes the integral self to be. The difference Theory declares itself to value comes in curiously fixed forms. Does a woman of color, embodying the virtue of "Difference" have no differences from another woman of color? Problems indeed proliferate: What about those others who are other than the Other with whom Theory groups them? Who are too diverse to accept the latest party line on diversity? Should they be proscribed as not black or not female enough? And what about some Other who is oppressed by some other Other?

Visible Sainthood

Theory's preferred subject positions are frozen in saintly postures, which brings us to another problem in Theory, that of its idealization of certain fetishized identities, the problem, as I shall call it, of visible saints. Here there is an American precedent for Theory, the American Puritan conceptualization of themselves as a community of visible saints. Catholic saints, in contrast, were impressive but singular and dead. John Cotton and other New England Puritans, with their pro- gressive American perfectionist spirit, were more expeditious. As Edmund Morgan, in *Visible Saints: The Story of a Puritan Idea*, recounts it:

> Though no human deserved salvation, God . . . had chosen to save a few, and to them He gave saving faith. They belonged to his real, his invisible church. To make the visible church as much as possible like the invisible, the later congregationalists argued that the visible church in admitting members should look for signs of saving faith. . . . Men, being human, would make mistakes, and the visible church would therefore remain only an approxima- tion of the invisible; but it should have in appearance the same purity that the invisible church had in reality; it should admit to membership only those who appeared to be saved. (34–35)

The Americans' radical conception shocked an English Puritan: "Samuel Hud- son . . . protested that 'Mr. *Cotton tels* us, that a *visible Church is a mysticall body, whereof . . . the Members* [are] *Saints and united together by a holy Covenant'* whereas this definition obviously belongs to the *'invisible Church'"* (Bercovitch, *The American Jere- miad*, 45).

Membership came to depend on a public testimony of the believer's expe- rience of receiving saving faith, followed by standing up to the congregation's cross-examination. This outlook may have created a somewhat propitious climate for invidious binary oppositions: "The church was to be 'a companie and fellowship of faithful and holie people.' The crucial question is what they meant by 'faithful and holie.' They answered in part by stating what they did not mean: outside the church were to be 'dogs and enchaunters, and Whoremongers, and Murderers, and Idolatours, and whosoever loveth and maketh lyes'" (Bercovitch, *The American Jeremiad*, 35).

It is self-evident that nothing could be easier than to make a case against the Puritans for their hegemonic self-privileging, for their stigmatizing of differ- ence and otherness, for the intolerance built into their very system of beliefs. But William Scheick noted, in 1971, the resemblance between the New Left and the Puritans: "What has occurred is that the Puritans' politics of religion has been transformed into the New Left's religion of politics, while the animating zeal behind both of them has remained nearly the same" ("New England Puritanism," 73). Carrying on from the New Left, some versions of Theory uncannily echo the structure of Puritan hegemony. They have visible saints, narrowly defined standards of admission into their congregation, and demonized Others, especially those so wicked as to believe differently. Like the Puritans, they believe in suppressing the discourse of the other, the resistant. They might consistently endorse Thomas Shepherd's heartfelt denunciation of the tolerance of incorrect views as "the foundation of all other Errors and abominations in the churches of God" (P. Miller, 122). Theory, then, has at least as fair a claim as the religious right to be in tune with a founding American religious discourse.

But there are problems with saintly identity, particularly when this identity is ascriptive and communal, based on membership in a community of belief. What about pretender saints? Puritans worried about religious hypocrisy, but the combination of ascriptive identity with visible sainthood has produced weirder possibilities of imposture. Henry Louis Gates recalls the praise lavished on the supposedly autobiographical Native American narrative Forrest Carter's *Education of Little Tree* until its author turned out to be a "white" former Klansman, whose previous major "text" was George Wallace's 1963 speech calling for " 'Segregation now . . . Segregation tomorrow . . . Segregation forever' " (1, 26–30). After the fact (but why only after?), *Little Tree* seems educative mainly about fantasies of the automatic benignity of subject positions. More recently, in Australia, the award-winning writer of a moving Aboriginal memoir, Wanda Koolmatrie, turned out to be actually Leon Carmen, white and male, while an acclaimed Aboriginal painter, Eddie Burrup, was revealed as Elizabeth Durack, an eighty-two-year-old woman of Irish descent (Spielmann, 11). Now, their previously acclaimed works are seen as trash, but why so? Was their talent only ascriptive to the work's presumed origin? For that matter, given how predictably the works "passed," would their ethnic representations have been fakes *even if* done by Aborigines? The epistemological privilege of minority subject position seems now so easily come by that one might suspect its real locale is in current political fantasy.

Moreover, can it be good for any group to think quite so well of itself as orthodox feminists do? Standpoint epistemology can become, to borrow Hilary Putnam's apothegm for Richard Rorty's relativism, "just solipsism with a 'we' instead of an 'I' " (ix), a form of group narcissism. Moreover, feminist sainthood can be problematic even for the saints. Feminists convincingly analyzed the Victorian "angel in the house" as an ideal that stifled women who attempted to live up to it and stigmatized those who did not. The rebels were not "real women." Now it is feminists who are casting women in idealized and stigmatized positions. Self-idealization necessitates repression, but there may be return of the repressed in those without the useful academic capacity for infinite abstraction. Rita Mae Brown, author of the celebrated lesbian novel, *Rubyfruit Jungle,* reflects that "out of that outburst [of anger at homophobia] on my part developed the whole ideology of the lesbian as the ultimate feminist and superior human being which I would like to say, many years later, is pure horseshit" (quoted in Echols, 69).

Some women of color, pressed into service as ascriptive visible saints by white American feminists, are growing restive: Anthony Appiah cites Sara Suleri as declaring herself "'heartily sick of being treated as an Otherness machine'" (157). Being a woman of color may prove as ultimately limiting as was the nineteenth-century ideal for (middle-class) women of the Angel in the Household. As a black historian declares, "Black people in the New Social History occupy a sacrosanct position; their actions cannot be queried. The intellectual position denies black people the freedom to be wrong" (C. Walker, xv). Perhaps, though certainly not consciously, the intellectual class needs the oppressed to stay in place so as to continue to serve as objects of exemplary discourse. But as Thomas Wentworth Higginson observed of *Uncle Tom's Cabin*, "'If it be the normal tendency of bondage to produce saints like Uncle Tom, let us all offer ourselves at auction immediately'" (cited by Fox-Genovese, 225).

Of course, the idealization of women, blacks, the "third world," etc., clearly has certain advantages for those groups "trading on the margin" (Green, 124–32) by way of "leveraged victimhood" (Falcoff, 15). It is no wonder that almost everyone in literary studies wants to be seen as marginal; the "margin" is, in fact, the center. Marginality is, in fact, the major form of academic capital—leading to literal capital—in English departments today. Thus it is understandable that the last thing women in the humanities want to interrogate is that they have recently *become* part of the hegemony in many leading-edge English departments. But since academic credit depends on the subject position of rebel or at least victim, their situation necessitates an elaborate game of Let's Pretend.

Identity politics, however, while it may yield local advantage, is in the long run an oxymoron. Theory disables the kinds of coalitions by which normal politics works, substituting their own utopian and ultimately totalist vision. It fantasizes bringing about revolutionary change by way of a cadre of English professors, a somewhat limited base, further narrowed to include only the most orthodox among feminists, Marxists, gays and lesbians, and persons of color. It is evident that a radical political coalition should include those who identify themselves in these terms; it is equally evident that a coalition limiting itself to them has little chance of bringing about even minor, much less utopian, change. But the Theory-speaking feminist cannot expand beyond her core constituency because, like Sylvia Plath's persona in "Fever 103," she can only reiterate, "I am too pure for you or anyone" (54).

One doubts that feminists such as Bauer can convert many not already true believers by a pedagogy based on the sanctification of women and the shaming of men. Iris Young argues that "'difference' politics" prevents a "politics of differ-ence," one that recognizes, and is prepared to mediate, felt differences. Young critiques the desire for pure, utopian unity in the self-constituted, ascriptively virtuous Other: "A desire for community in feminist groups . . . helps reproduce their homogeneity" (301). The tendency "denies difference in the concrete sense of making it difficult for people to respect those with whom they do not identify" and leads to "denying or suppressing differences within political groups or movements" (311–12). The utopian demand for total, instant renovation of "Western" society "detemporalizes its understanding of social change by positing the desired society as the complete negation of existing society" (302), whereas "if institutional change is possible at all, it must begin from intervening in the contradictions and tensions of existing society. No telos of the final society exists, moreover; society understood as a moving and contradictory process implies that change for the better is always possible and always necessary" (315).

But this is to miss the point. Much of what passes for politics in Theory is the rhetorical game of demonstrating personal perfection through identification with an ascriptively righteous group. The politics of subject position has less to do with political change in the real world than posturings in a symbolic world of ascriptive positions of saint and demon. It is the politics of ascriptive, unearned self-esteem and of resentment of all outside the orthodox, fetishized self-defined saintly community.

4

Discourse Radicalism

A curious aspect of Theory is its condemnation of *an entire mode of literature,* realism, not for what given realists say but as inherently conservative and oppressive in its *form.* Realism has become the straight white male of literary forms.

Why this aversion to literary realism? Theory's metaphysical base is in philosophical idealism—which it oddly terms "materialism"—and idealism is naturally at odds with metaphysical realism while metaphysical realism underlies literary realism. But I believe the real basis for the intensity of Theory's aversion to realism is in its aversion to reality. Reality, as we have seen, has been a disappointment. Not only has it not measured up to the dreams of Theory, but it has falsified them in every possible respect—except one. In the world of pure discourse, Theory reigns supreme. A generation of graduate students has been taught that since there is no "truth" they should simply accept the dogmas of "progressive" ideology. Instead of having to do the labor-intensive work of close reading, one can do appliqué criticism: "evaluating cultural phenomena as historically progressive or regressive" (Graff, 173). In Theory doubt functions as a universal methodological principle relating to all discourse when it is deployed against the opposition but is silently dropped for what Theory advocates. Truth is "relative" only in relation to political convenience.

Discourse radicalism combines deconstruction with Marxism or feminism or both to accuse whole genres of literature of oppressing designated minorities. It declares that any form of literature that represents reality is propagandizing for the preservation of the sociopolitical status quo by trying to pass off a social construction as natural and therefore valid. This variant of Theory descends obviously from Foucault's concept of discourse but owes even more to another French theorist, Roland Barthes. Barthes's *Mythologies* "deconstructs" the ideology encoded in mass discourse running from advertisements to wrestling (seen as a semiotic discourse). But in a methodological essay, "Myth Today," Barthes gives away *his* mythology.

The idea that carries through *Mythologies,* borrowed from Marx's *German Ideology,* is that bourgeois myth mystifies historical and cultural products into eternal natural essences. Barthes's deconstructions of various discourses unmask the rhetoric and semiotics of this transformation. Where his argument becomes fuzzy is in his attempt to show that "revolutionary language proper cannot be mythical" (*Mythologies*, 146). But is not *proper* revolutionary language a weasel word, allowing Barthes to exclude most of what passes for revolutionary language? He goes on to assert that it is the openly political nature of "revolutionary language" that keeps it myth-free: "It is because it generates speech which is *fully*, that is to say initially and finally, political, and not, like myth, speech which is initially political and finally natural, that revolution excludes myth . . . The bourgeoisie hides the fact that it is the bourgeoisie and thereby produces myth; revolution announces itself openly as revolution and thereby abolishes myth" (146). The idea seems to be that revolutionary language is self-evidently real and needs no hegemonical masks. But how do we recognize such language? Barthes gives not a single example, though he has deluged us with horrible examples of bourgeois myth. I think Barthes's uncharacteristic reticence comes from being unable to find undiscrediting examples.

Barthes does admit there are myths on the Left but only "inasmuch, precisely, as the Left is not revolution" (*Mythologies*, 146). "Precisely" is rich here, functioning as a linguistic assertion of an exactness and groundedness otherwise quite absent from his argument. Looked at outside an unexamined agreement with Barthes's politics, is not Barthes's language here "precisely" functioning as Left mythology? Indeed, the entire argument of *Mythologies* is an elegant presentation of an essentialist Left mythology: that politics is the ground of existence, that everything is politics. Let me clarify the issue because it is a favorite Theory maneuver to claim that Theory is overt in its politics, whereas aesthetically inclined criticism encodes them covertly. But one can be a primarily aesthetic or ethical critic without in any way denying that it is possible to interpret the same work from a political perspective. The real question is whether the *essence* of everything is political. Here is another example of Theory denying essentialism on principle while covertly practicing it.

What can Barthes mean by saying that "Left-wing myth supervenes precisely at the moment when revolution changes itself into 'the Left,' that is, when it accepts to wear a mask, to hide its name, to generate an innocent metalanguage and to distort itself into 'Nature'" (*Mythologies*, 146–47). My best guess is that since he mentions Stalin later in this paragraph he means that the revolution changes itself into "the Left" when it either becomes institutionalized into a state or into an opposition party. This implies that authentic revolution must be permanent, a position that was termed "infantile leftism" by Lenin and that, when put into practice in Mao's "cultural revolution," proved an unqualified disaster for China.

Barthes goes on to argue that *"Left-wing myth is inessential"* (*Mythologies*, 147) compared to right-wing myth, declaring that "there are no 'Left-wing' myths concerning marriage, cooking, the home, the theater, the law, morality, etc." (147). But his own discourse contradicts him since *Mythologies*, in countering right-wing myths of all the above, is implicitly constructing left-wing myths of marriage, etc., especially in seeing their only meanings to be political. Moreover, Chinese and Soviet Communist myths of all that Barthes mentions are not far to seek. Even if Barthes's argument were accurate, he forgets that in communist regimes hegemony is less necessary since the state controls the dissemination of information and the police and the army can be called on to take care of unauthorized voices.

The moral force of Barthes's argument and of Theory generally is that of exposé—the unmasking of deceptive rhetoric used to erase history and cover up structures of oppression. But it is the Marxist Left when in power that has made the most extraordinary advances in historical erasure and public lying. The Czechoslovakian novelist Milan Kundera gives an instance from February 1948 when Klement Gottwald, the head of the newly triumphant Czechoslovakian Communist Party, stepped out on the balcony of a Baroque palace in Prague to address a grateful nation:

> Gottwald was flanked by his comrades, with Clementis standing next to him. There were some snow flurries, it was cold, and Gottwald was bareheaded. The solicitous Clementis took off his own fur cap and set it on Gottwald's head.
>
> The party propaganda section put out hundreds of thousands of copies of a photograph of that balcony with Gottwald, a fur cap on his head and comrades at his side, speaking to the nation. . . . Every child knew the photograph from posters, schoolbooks, and museums.
>
> Four years later Clementis was charged with treason and hanged. The propaganda section immediately airbrushed him out of history and, obviously, out of all the photographs as well. Ever since, Gottwald has stood on that balcony alone. Where Clementis once stood, there is only bare wall. All that remains of Clementis is the cap on Gottwald's head. (*Book of Laughter,* 3)

David King, in *The Commissar Vanishes: The Falsification of Photographs and Art in Stalin's Russia,* documents with archival photographic evidence the communist practice of airbrushing people out of history.

The consequences of Left lying can be horrific, as shown in Jasper Becker's account of how the great Chinese famine caused by Mao's administrative blunders as well as Mao's political survival of it were a function of a totalitarian structural falsity:

> Mao could not be brought down because he had created a world in which all beliefs and judgements were suspended. No one dared move or act according to what he knew to be true. Instead, even the highest-ranking officials moved in a secretive society paralysed by an all-pervasive network of informers and

spies. In a world of distorting mirrors, it became hard to grasp that such senseless cruelties were even taking place. The grotesque efforts that some officials made to deceive . . . almost defies imagination. Who could believe that Party officials would plaster and paint trees stripped of their bark by starving peasants to hide a famine? (311–12)

After Mao's death, the famine was memorialized in a Henan Province opera "called *Huang Ho* or *Catastrophe of Lies*" (112).

It is fair to ask whether Barthes himself is talking the language of revolution or the mythology of the Left. Before his passages above Barthes tries to define revolutionary language, but he does so in primarily *literary* terms. Some whole forms of language, he argues, are less resistant to myth than others: "Articulated language, which is most often robbed by myth, offers little resistance" (*Mythologies*, 131). The closer language approaches to "the zero degree" of signification, the better it resists myth (132). Poetry, especially modernist experimental poetry, might seem to evade myth better since "it wants to be an anti-language" and it "always asserts itself as a murder of language, a kind of spatial tangible analogue of silence" but "the apparent lack of order of signs, which is the poetic facet of an essential order, is captured by myth, and transformed into an empty signifier, which will serve to *signify* poetry," a fetishization that delivers it a fortiori to myth (133–34). But Flaubert in *Bouvard and Pécuchet* does succeed in delivering "an archeological restoration of a given mythical speech" and is thus "counter-mythical" (136).

Even granting these by no means proven propositions, there is something of a disconnect between literary and political revolution. Barthes admits a problem in the best example he could find:

Flaubert's great merit (and that of all artificial mythologies . . .) is that he gave to the problem of realism a frankly semiological solution. True, it is a somewhat incomplete merit, for Flaubert's ideology, since the bourgeois was for him only an aesthetic eyesore, was not at all realistic. But at least he avoided the major sin in literary matters, which is to confuse ideological with semiological reality. (*Mythologies*, 136)

This is what we now call postmodernism, where the fictiveness of representation is overt, the main significance. But postmodernist writers tend toward anarchism and nihilism more than toward revolution. And if they are not influenced toward revolution by their writings, it needs explanation why their readers would be. But then to link revolutionary literary language to revolutionary political ventures is a category error, two functionally different discourses united only by a common word. T. S. Eliot in his time was a revolutionary in poetic form, but the Left has yet to claim him.

Is not Barthes himself an aesthetic revolutionary rather than a political one? Indeed, are his revolutionary claims not part of a thrilling aesthetic, antibourgeois pose, the form dandyism took in mid-nineteenth-century Paris? In *Mythologies* and in *S/Z* Barthes tries to deconstruct realism into a system of clichés, but his choice of the Left was the prescribed one for French intellectuals of his era, an embodied cliché. His was a doctrinal discourse radicalism, a form of radicalism easily institutionalized and eminently teachable in universities. Its main doctrine was antirealism: "It is well known how often our 'realistic' literature is mythical (if only as a crude myth of realism) and how our 'literature of the unreal' has at least the merit of being only slightly so. The wise thing would of course be to define the writer's realism as an essentially ideological problem" (137). He then prescriptively asserts that "one must deal with the writer's realism either as an ideological substance . . . or as a semiological value" (137), thus setting up the research program followed by an abundance of soi-disant radical English professors.

Literary realism became a discursive culprit by having "real" in it. In politically virtuous literature, language has supposedly wised up, referring not to "reality" (always in scare quotes) but only to itself. Following Barthes's prescription, signifiers defer eternally to other signifiers and never grossly proposition a signified.

A perfect example of discourse radicalism is in Catherine Belsey's *Critical Practice* and her essays along the same line. Belsey's book is a Theory classic, written in 1980, still in print in paperback, used as a text in critical courses and frequently cited. Belsey proposes that "it follows from Saussure's theory of language as a system of differences that the world is intelligible only in discourse: there is no unmediated experience, no access to the raw reality of self and others" ("Constructing the Subject," 596). Thus: "If we accept that it is the linguistic system of differences which articulates the world of things and ideas, how can we claim that one discourse is more 'scientific' than another?" (*Critical Practice*, 63). Further:

> The subject is constructed in language and in discourse and, since the symbolic order in its discursive use is closely related to ideology, in ideology. It is in this sense that ideology has the effect, as Althusser argues, of constituting individuals as subjects, and it is also in this sense that their subjectivity appears "obvious." Ideology suppresses the role of language in the construction of the subject. As a result, people "recognize" (misrecognize) themselves in the way in which ideology "interpellates" them, or in other words, addresses them as subjects, calls them by their names and in turn "recognizes" their autonomy. As a result . . . they "willingly" adopt the subject positions necessary to their participation in the social formation. . . . In patriarchal society women "choose" to do the housework, to make sacrifices for their children, not to become engineers. ("Constructing the Subject," 596)

What we take for reality is merely a set of conventions.

This discourse, though breathtaking in how much it doubts, does have faith in the superior reality of language. As she quotes Lacan: "'It is the world of words that creates the world of things'" (*Critical Practice*, 136). It is true that bridges are built according to specifications and that even the numbers used to calculate are words. These constitute the scientific discourse of engineering. But the creation of the bridge in accordance with this discourse must answer to nonverbal physical realities of balance, stress, and so on. The words in the specifications describing those realities had better be accurate. This necessity is independent of the gender and race of the engineer. Who becomes an engineer can be an ideological question and the uses to which the bridge is put is a political question, but the sociology and politics of engineering have nothing to do with the *scientific* determinants of whether the bridge stays up. In relation to keeping the bridge up, the discourse of engineering specifications is "more 'scientific' than another." Practically applied scientific discourse is distinctive precisely because it is continually monitored by sometimes ultimate forms of reality testing, and it is doubtful that even Belsey would wish that discourse be replaced by Theory were she walking over that bridge.

On all other questions she would, for she has true faith in Theory and all its infallible ways. As in how the Marxist critic Macherey shows the process by which authors produce texts: "Criticism is the *science* which offers a *knowledge* of the mode of production and so, finally, *a knowledge of history*" (*Critical Practice*, 138; my emphasis). And: "In *reality*, when Barthes reads *Sarrasine* he transforms it by the application of *existing forms of knowledge*, employing post-Saussurean linguistics, Lacanian psychoanalysis and Marxist economic theory to produce a meaning which was literally not available to Balzac and his contemporary readers" (139). All this Belsey presents as Truth and Reality, somehow mysteriously transcending the problem that "language is a system of differences with no positive terms" ("Constructing the Subject," 595).

The validation Belsey's discourse offers for itself is to name its sacred origins: Marx, Saussure, Barthes, Lacan, and especially Althusser who functions as its Moses descending from the mountains with the tables of the law. These authorities thoroughly interpellate Belsey's discourse. This does, in a way, illustrate her theory: It is not Belsey who speaks in "her" text but authoritarian Marxist and poststructuralist discourse.

Realism, Belsey believes, is in alliance with liberal humanism in assuming "a world of non-contradictory (and therefore fundamentally unalterable) individuals whose unfettered consciousness is the origin of meaning, knowledge and action" ("Constructing the Subject," 599). Her discourse's animus against realism, then, is that it interpellates people in the wrong direction: "Ideology interpellates concrete individuals as subjects, and bourgeois ideology in particular emphasizes the fixed identity of the individual. . . . In these circumstances, how is it possible to suppose that . . . we are ourselves capable of change, and therefore capable both of acting to change the social formation and of transforming ourselves to constitute a new kind of society?" (597). The other society it means seems fairly evident. So the awful thing about realist literature (and apprehending reality generally) is that it prevents us all from becoming Marxist socialists. Otherwise we would rush for that social formation like lemmings to the coastline.

    Another of our bourgeois myths is the naive notion that books are written by authors:

> The author's name on the cover, known, established, famous, is the guarantee of access to his or her imagination, just as the brand name on the product is the name of the employer or the company, not of the workers whose labors produced it. In a similar way, the author's name evokes given essences, qualities of insight and understanding, and not the labour of producing out of the available signifying systems of language and literature an intelligible fiction. (Belsey, *Critical Practice*, 127)

In other words, the author, like the company owner, takes the credit for the real work done by . . . who? Was not the labor of putting together the signifying systems done by the author? If what Belsey means is that books do not magically emerge but are written over a period of time by authors using the signifying systems of language to write them, that is not quite news. She seems to want to say in more forthright Derridean fashion that it is the signifying system that does the work while the exploitative author takes the credit. But lacking the courage of her confusions she resorts to grammatical obfuscations to cover up her contradictions.

    After explaining what is wrong with authors, the discourse sets out to defeat them by attributing any sign of intelligence within a text to a reified notion of the text itself. But the text, like the writer, is a neurotic pretender:

> The realist text is a determinate representation, an intelligible structure which claims to convey intelligible relationships between its elements. In its attempt to create a coherent and internally consistent fictive world the text, in spite of itself, exposes incoherencies, omissions, absences, and transgressions which in turn reveal the inability of the language of ideology to create coherence. This becomes apparent because the contradiction between the diverse elements drawn from the different discourses, the ideological project and the literary form, creates an absence at the centre of the work. (Belsey, "Constructing the Subject," 603)

Theory fills in this center.

In so doing it becomes the *real* author of the text. Belsey has warned us that "expressive-realist criticism is finally parasitic on literature, unable to distance itself from literature to the point where it has an independent process of production to perform" (*Critical Practice*, 127). There is a better way:

> The solution, then, must be not only a new mode of writing but also a new critical practice which insists on finding the plurality, however "parsimonious," of the text and refuses the pseudo-dominance constructed by the forms of classic realism. . . . A form of criticism which refuses to reproduce the pseudo-knowledge offered by the text provides a real knowledge of the work of literature. . . . Such a criticism finds in the literary work a new object of intelligibility: it produces the text. (129)

So the real author of all those realist works is none other than Catherine Belsey's discourse. It has gone well beyond the classical economic era parasitism of those ancillary critics who try sympathetically to determine the author's meaning. Rather, it mirrors late capitalist rapacity in its hostile takeover of the text.

Belsey's cultural reproduction of Theory and her application of it to a leveraged buyout of reality is almost too perfect an example of Theory. Where to begin? For one, it offers a perfect illustration of grid criticism: Read any book as she does and you will get the same meanings. One is reminded of the character in a Nancy Mitford novel who "read only one book in my life, and that is *White Fang*. It's so frightfully good I've never bothered to read another" (*Pursuit of Love*, chapter 9, 91).

Of course, the root problem is Belsey's unquestioning faith in discourse radicalism, a wholly untenable theory. All that follows from it is, as the lawyers say, fruits of a poisoned tree. Even if logocentrism was the major tendency in "Western" philosophy as poststructuralism wrongly claims, it fails to account for oppression in countries neither Western nor capitalist, most notably communist ones. Moreover, Belsey supposes herself to be philosophically materialist but only by the maneuver of defining her linguistic idealism as a form of materialism. Leonard Jackson notes, "The modern 'materialist' is often somebody who believes that the class struggle is a contest over the control of the production of new meanings for literary texts" (*Poverty of Structuralism*, 4).

The "production" of the text for which Belsey's discourse celebrates itself is as easy as it is arbitrary. Yet it is contradicted by its own premises. Belsey, following Althusser, identifies ideology with intelligibility: That is why ideology is inescapable. But Belsey's discourse claims to see through ideology by discerning its contradictions. But what gives Belsey the access to these contradictions? How can you see a contradiction except from some ground above it? If that ground is another ideology, then one is, *by the very logic of Theory*, still within the circle of mystifications, especially if her positions are intelligible. For Belsey to call *her* ideology "science" begs the question. So if Belsey's discourse is right, it must be wrong.

The discourse is wrong not only in its premises, that is, in general, but in its reading of real realist novels, that is, in particular. If it understood realist fiction, it could not say that the story of classical realism "moves inevitably toward *closure* which is also disclosure, the dissolution of enigma through the reestablishment of order, recognizable as a reinstatement or a development of the order which is understood to have preceded the events of the story itself." Nor that "the moment of closure is the point at which the events of the story become fully intelligible to the reader." Nor that "classic realism cannot foreground contradiction" (Belsey, *Critical Practice*, 70, 82).

In the real as well as realist world, the conclusions of Henry James's fictions upset the readers of his and our times with their ambiguities. Where might Belsey find closure in *The Turn of the Screw*? So far various casebooks employing various modes of criticism, including Theory, have been unable to. Does Belsey suppose Isabel Archer to be a character unable to change? Many classic realist texts work precisely by pulling the reader into an agon of competing crucial ethical choices in a situation precluding guarantees. Realism is best read through Wolfgang Iser's concept of "gaps of indeterminacy" created by characters who engage but never satisfactorily close with moral realities that cannot quite be abstractly and determinately named. The novel thus "discloses its attitudes through degrees of negation, thwarting the reader's expectations and stimulating him to reflection, which in turn creates a counterbalance to the negativity of the text" (46). Far from confirming ideological expectations, the realist novel forces the reader "to exercise his own critical faculties in order to relieve his distress by uncovering potential alternatives arising out of the world he has read about" (113–14). "The reader is constantly forced to think in terms of alternatives, as the only way in which he can avoid the unambiguous and suspect position of the characters is to visualize the possibilities they have not thought of" (118). Characters are less likely to "interpellate" the reader than serve as imperfect or horrible examples, inviting not a passive response but highly active moral and cultural work.

For Martha Nussbaum, the "novel as genre is committed, in its very structure and in the structure of its relationship with its reader, to the pursuit of uncertainties and vulnerabilities . . . of the human form of life" (390). This uncertainty has a major epistemological dimension, as in *The Turn of the Screw* and in Isabel Archer's confrontation of realities that contradict her conception of the world. A central technique of realism is the play with opposing signs or even sign systems as in *Portrait of a Lady* where Isabel Archer and Gilbert Osmond use the same terms but mean diametrically different things by them.

A major convention in realist fiction is its unmasking of conventions, its defining itself against various rhetorical, hegemonical discourses of unreality, as in the deromanticization of war fiction by Stephen Crane and of Southern fantasies of happy slaves singing in the field by Harriet Beecher Stowe. Iris Murdoch suggests that the freedom the realist novel seeks is "the freedom *from* fantasy" (*Sovereignty of Good*, 66; my emphasis). But what specifies the realist novel is how it folds the epistemological question into the existential one.

The question is not whether ethics is a mere epistemic imposition but of the need for a particular ethical choice, immediate and existentially binding, in a highly ambiguous and conflicted situation. What makes problems "real" is that they represent, in however mediated a fashion, problems readers themselves encounter in their relationships with lovers, spouses, siblings, children, and parents in situations that force choices about matters both quotidian and ultimate—where to live, with whom, on what, at what psychological price and social cost. It is observable that readers find such problems more troubling than whether a given scene in a postmodern novel is to be apprehended as real or as a joke of the novelist to foreground literary artifice. Of course, unreliable narrators can be found in realist texts as well but with a different effect and affect—more like the question of whether you can trust your spouse or whether your child's philosophy of life derives from a controlled substance.

I am *not* arguing that reality or realist literature is self-evident, something *no serious realist would propose,* though this is the straw man Theory sets in opposition to its own antirealism. Reality, like the moral truth it quests after, is elusive. In Iris Murdoch's formulation, "Good is indefinable . . . because of the infinite difficulty of the task of apprehending a magnetic but inexhaustible reality. . . . If apprehension of good is apprehension of the individual and the real then good partakes of the infinite elusive character of reality" (*Sovereignty of Good*, 42). Reality, so conceived, is more likely to be painful rather than wish fulfilling. The title of a Wislawa Szymborska poem is in the realist key: "In Praise of Feeling Bad about Yourself" (124). What makes realist texts good for moral thinking is their antitheoretical presentation of a world we never made, one characterized by an obdurate contingency. The "New Realist" painter Philip Pearlstein notes, "Reality is not something I chose but something I found myself in" (quoted in Shi, 306).

Belsey's is only the most emphatic statement of the dogma that characters in fiction are purely textual effects, reflecting the culture's ideology, not human reality or moral personhood. For Belsey, characters function solely to interpellate readers by way of preconceived ideology. On the contrary, it is not only possible but enabling to perceive characters in fiction as reflecting the reality of human being-in-the-world by playing out various ethical and psychological possibilities. Readers validly can share an author's ethical perception of characters, who convincingly represent not ideological positions primarily but people not unlike ourselves. Indeed, the true absurdity lies in denials that this can be so and in unearned privilegings of textuality over reality.

Our experience as readers is that writers enable ethical—and political—rethinking through the characterization of believable individuals. The study of literature educates us "in how to picture and understand human situations" (Murdoch, *Sovereignty of Good*, 34). But how could this be so? Is it not obvious that characters are made up of words? How then could they reflect reality? But if words do not reflect reality, what of importance is being said when "capitalists" or "white males" are accused of "oppression"? If reference is an illusion, this must go all the way up and all the way down, rather than being a conceptual weapon with which to bash the "bourgeois," and conveniently put back in the armory when a "progressive" writer or character puts in her claim. Surely Margaret MacDonald is right when she argues that Jane Austen's Emma as not merely "identical with the words by which she is created. Emma is a 'character.' As such, she can, in appropriate senses, be called charming, generous, foolish, and even 'lifelike.' No one could sensibly use these epithets of words" (66–67). Surely it is evident to all but the theoretically blind that we match our experience of characters with our experience of persons. This is not a static relation; as our experience widens or is transformed utterly, so is our view of character and the books they are in. In contrast, Belsey's matching of characters with a rigid ideological system is static indeed.

The ethical meaningfulness of literature is that its ethical dilemmas are typical, particular, unpredictable, and situational. They are representative but too particularized to be resolved by ethical abstractions and rules. Hugh Bredin is right in saying: "Falstaff's laughter is not that of Iago. Don Quixote's indignation is not that of Hamlet" (298). Authentic ethical discourse is thus casuistical. This was Kant's view, though the mythology of philosophy holds him to have believed in a rigidified set of rules. As Ralph C. S. Walker points out, the second part of the *Metaphysics of Morals* "is full of what [Kant] calls 'casuistical questions.' 'Casuistical' has no negative connotation here. It implies that the questions can only be answered by careful thinking about the particular case, and not just by deploying rules" (10).

Bakhtin believed that "novels offer our richest portraits of real situations and constitute our greatest repository of ethical wisdom" because "they focus on the particularities of each specific situation, all those momentous specificities on which informed ethical choice depends. In the root sense of the term, Bakhtin's approach to ethics was casuistical in that he believed there to be no substitute for an educated sensitivity to individual *cases*" (Morson, 224).

This is how, as Martin Price shows, "all novels serve in some measure as a testing of values, an exploration of what their realization costs or confers" (16). Novels reflect the conflicted situations of ethical forced options:

To discern those principles which govern the novelist's creation of a set of asymmetrical characters requires delicacy and tact, almost as much as governed the creation in the first place. For the complexity of relationships corresponds precisely to the complexity of the principles that the novelist, however consciously, has embodied in them. One finds oneself saying, "not this, but somewhat more like that," "not quite, but almost," "in this respect but not in that." (17)

In the realist world, general ideas are judged by how well they explain partic- ularities. In Theory World, as Belsey's discourse so well illustrates, particularities are proscribed for failure to conform to Theory wish fulfillment. It is not the closure and determinacy of realist fiction that is the problem for Theory but its sense of contingency and unpredictability as opposed to the political certainties of Theory. George Eliot proclaimed, in the realist novel *Middlemarch*: "There is no general doctrine which is not capable of eating out our morality if unchecked by the deep-seated habit of direct fellow-feeling with individual fellow-men" (chapter 61, 429).

Particularity goes with a respect for other minds. As paradoxical as it may sound, this respect extends even to the realist novelist's respect for her own cre- ations. Anne Tyler's experience is that sometimes characters "simply won't obey you. . . . Where did those little paper people get so much power?" (cited in Michaels, 46). She recalls that she received furious phone calls from readers who wanted Jeremy and Mary to have stayed together in *Celestial Navigation*: "All along I wanted that ending too, and I was sure I'd be able to work out a way. I kept pushing toward it, but that writing felt wooden: my sentences were jerky when I looked back at them. In a way I felt that I was trying to cover up a lie, and then I thought, I may as well tell the truth: the woman leaves the man" (55).

Belsey's real complaint against realist novels may be that they do not serve as advertisements for the "progressive" agenda. In fact, she is wrong even about her putative allies. In fact, most feminist fiction—Marge Piercy's work, for instance—is realist in genre, conventional in style. It is surprising that this should be surpris- ing. George Watson reminds us of the observation of the leftist leader Ferdinand Lassalle: "As Lassalle once remarked, the most revolutionary act is, and always remains, to say out loud what is" (55).

Though there are important experimentalist women and minority writers, most, even most feminists, choose realism. Jay Clayton entitles a chapter in his book on contemporary American fiction, "The Narrative Turn in Minority Writ- ing," pointing out that most social radical writing finds narration its best means of moving the reader (93). He cites Toni Morrison: "'People *crave* narration. . . . That's the way they learn things'" (95). Additionally, Clayton notes, "By showing rather than telling, narrative may escape the processes that recuperate or coopt more explicit forms of writing" (98).

In contrast, Belsey's discourse is nothing if not explicit. Stylistically and ar- gumentatively its writing resolutely contradicts its poststructuralist prescriptions, never risking the unexpected, never wandering into play, never showing rather than telling. As a result, it is thoroughly recuperated and co-opted by Theory.

Women may most frequently write realism not only to reach a wider audience but because of an elective affinity. Sir Walter Scott admitted as much: "'The women do this better—Edgeworth, Ferrier, Austen have all had their portraits of real society, far superior to anything Man, vain Man, has produced of the like nature" (quoted in Tuttleton, 29). Perhaps this does stem from a superior epistemological standpoint, women having, perhaps, a better sense of the contingent details of quotidian life. If so, they might have an affinity for literary realism.

For that matter, the definitional lines between realism, modernism, and post-modernism are more distinct to critics than to writers. Was Dos Passos's *Manhattan Transfer* realist, naturalist, modernist, or postmodernist? Could it, as I think, be reasonably described as all the above? But critics have an investment in termino-logical trends. This is evident in Ramon Saldivar's *Chicano Narrative: The Dialectics of Difference*. Saldivar argues for a canon of Chicano writers that is structured by their relation to Marxism and French poststructuralism. Catholicism enters in only as something to be discredited as quickly as possible—it is not in Saldivar's index. Richard Rodriguez is included only so Saldivar can argue for his exclusion as a horrible example of a Mexican American who is not a true Chicano since he has an identity that fails to match with Saldivar's Marxist, deconstructionist grid. Specific Chicano ethnic identity seems then to depend on the thought of Marx and Derrida.

The poststructuralism Saldivar imputes to Chicano writers is, in some in-stances, more a production of *Chicano Narrative*'s critical practice than a property of the texts. At points this critical productivity is overt, as when it announces that "if read dialectically and across the grain of its represented terms" (180), a certain passage yields the discourse Saldivar thinks proper for Chicanos. Saldivar praises a narrative for consisting "almost entirely of women's voices, speaking the concerns of being in the everyday world, giving expression to the concrete realities of ev-eryday life" (177–78). This sounds like realism, but Saldivar *calls it* postmodernism. Similarly Saldivar declares that "read dialectically, narratives indicate that language and discourse do affect human life in determining ways, ways that are themselves shaped by social history. Giving rise to questions concerning language itself, the sovereignty of our identity, and the laws that govern our behavior, they reveal the heterogeneous systems that resist the formation of a unitary base of truth" (207). Doubtless, but what is specific to Chicano literature about all this, which is exactly what such bourgeois humanists as Ian Watt and Erich Auerbach said of the realist canon generally?

For *Chicano Narrative*, however, the "masterworks of the dominant literary cul-ture are the dialogical negations of the marginal texts not sanctioned by the hege-monic culture" (Saldivar, 214). If these reifications are not intended to summon up the ghost of Walt Whitman to proleptically oppress Sandra Cisneros, the discourse must mean to indict the cultural uses of the masterworks rather than the works themselves. But this is no more self-evident *or* argued than the rest of its case. Could it not be that some canonical writers were *enabling* for Chicano writers, as theorists of literary hybridity—the doubly enabling interchange between "mainstream" and minority literature—argue?

An example of the dialectics of difference is how Richard Rubio, the protagonist of José Antonio Villareal's *Pocho*, "will consistently choose not to choose" and asserts that "herein lies Richard's generic difference" (62), but here Saldivar appears to be unaware that he has echoed the main line of interpretation of the "mainstream" American romance (Joel Porte, Michael Davitt Bell, Edgar Dryden). In writing about Tomas Rivera's brilliant novel, *Y no se lo trago la tierra*, he does not recognize that Rivera's sophisticated use of metonymy, by which, supposedly because he is Chicano, he departs from his ground base of realism (88), is a staple of John Dos Passos's fiction from *Manhattan Transfer* on. Was Dos Passos able to be postmodernist before the term because his father was Portuguese? The "mainstream," to which Saldivar opposes his construction of a deconstructive Marxist "Chicano" canon, is, arguably, at least as deconstructive, and some of it, notably *Manhattan Transfer*, as radical.

Other Theory assertions recur, such as that capitalism "institutionalizes male sexual dominance and female sexual submission" (197). Saldivar praises Cherrié Moraga for avoiding ideological interpellation by patriarchy though arguably she has been interpellated with Marxist ideology (195–96). And finally there is the ultimate poststructuralist claim:

> The notion of a positive, central identity is the bedrock of hegemonic bourgeois-humanist ideological systems because a fixed identity can be persuaded, coerced, and ultimately, controlled. An unfixed, decentered identity alters the pattern by which a society must position the subject so that "it shall freely submit to its subjection" [Althusser]. (174)

One of the Theory concepts I examine in my next chapter is the unreflective association of personal integrity, the relatively centered self, with subjection. I suggest that Theory has it backward.

5

A Ruthless Criticism
of Everything Existing

Theory is most self-contradictory in its overt negations and covert resurrections of value. Theory thrills by its ruthless negations, using the methodological short-cuts examined in previous chapters. Other discourses are discredited for violating essential rules of thought by being essentialist—that is, centered, universalist, transcendent. These bad discourses are also ascriptively discredited by illegitimate origins: "white, bourgeois, androcentric Westerners" (Harding, "Feminism," 101). At its boldest Theory seems to follow Marx's attack on every aspect of his world: "If the designing of the future and the proclamation of ready-made solutions for all time is not our affair, then we have to realize all the more clearly what we have to accomplish in the present—I am speaking of a *ruthless criticism of everything existing*" ("For a Ruthless Criticism," 13).

Yet Theory, the Marxist version most of all, recuperates the transcendent center that it claims to have unmasked with its own proper transcendent center, constituted not just generally as politics but specifically by a Left politics presented as self-evident. This is the procedure of Frederic Jameson's *The Political Unconscious* where Jameson claims that it is only through an "ideal" central standpoint that the partiality of the codes of traditional criticism are revealed: "Their juxtaposition with a dialectical or totalizing, properly Marxist ideal of understanding will be used to demonstrate the structural limitations of the other interpretive codes, and, in particular to show the 'local' ways in which they construct their objects of study and the 'strategies of containment' whereby they are able to project the illusion that their readings are somehow complete and self-sufficient." Marxist criticism "subsumes" rival readings, thus centering them in Marxism. Yet there is something admittedly missing: "The reader should not . . . expect anything like that exploratory projection of what a vital and emergent political culture should be and do" (10). Politics are not immediate and negotiable but metaphysical and utopian: to conceive "those new forms of collective thinking and collective culture which lie beyond the boundaries of our own world" (11). The subject at hand, however, is to analyze "the construction of the bourgeois subject in emergent capitalism and its schizophrenic disintegration in our own time" (12).

For Jameson, clearly, Marxist political ideology recuperates the center vacated by the discrediting of the personal self and literary work: "Only the [Marxist] dialectic provides a way for 'decentering' the subject concretely, and for transcending the 'ethical' in the direction of the political and the collective" (60). But this implies a self centered *in* a version of the political, one which Jameson finds it unnecessary to justify by argument though it is the ground for criticizing all else that exists.

Jameson sees his substitution as self-evident, but if deconstructionist thought validates the scare quotes around "ethical," what justifies their absence for "political" and "collective"? What makes "politics" an indubitable transcendent center? Whose politics? Whose collective? Do these transcendent categories of Theory actually transcend even the narrow precincts of university humanities departments?

In this chapter I propose a recuperation of self and of literary work from the unearned negations of Theory. I also propose that the political self may be at least as liable to deconstruction in ethical and personal terms as ethics and selfhood are in political terms. If one's selfhood and ethics can be relativized as merely epiphenomenal of one's political subject position, why cannot one's political subject position be relativized as merely epiphenomenal of one's selfhood and ethics? It is not self-evident how the reduction of the self to a political party line endows it with a superior standpoint.

Theory assumes that the decentered self is joyously freed of the binding limitations of the bourgeois construction of self. But Jameson declares this battle already won; the bourgeois subject has dissolved into "schizophrenic disintegration." Even if this be true—some doubt seems possible—is Theory correct in its assertion that schizophrenic disintegration is good for us, even just politically good?

Consumerist Freeplay

Present-day American capitalism has obvious imbalances and dysfunctions. Some of these are an inordinate and growing gap in income between the few and the many, the disappearance of work in the urban ghetto (see William Julius Wilson— although recently work appears to be resurfacing in the ghetto), and the encroachment of capitalism on social, educational, spiritual, and aesthetic realms wherein the market economy simply is not an adequate measure of value. But whether or not Theory contributes to these dysfunctions, it seems little to the purpose in resisting and changing them. Its contempt for ethics and transcendence disables what we most need to rediscover: an ethical balance. Many of us support restraints from the market and governmental supplements for values, artistic and compassionate, that the market ignores. Theory, however, calls not for amelioration of the market economy but for an uncompromised rejection of it. But the only known systemic alternative to the market is the Marxist socialist polity that led to "the most colossal case of political carnage in history" (Malia, 3). If Marxist socialism, meaning the replacement of the market with a centrally organized command economy, is not what "progressives" advocate, they owe us a clearer explanation. Calling, evidently, for the ruinous economics and politics that have characterized Marxist socialist practice, Theory despises the personal, ethical energy needed to resist the reduction of all value to commodity value. For instance, Theory's politicized readings are mostly (not always) blind to the resistances and alternatives encoded in "classic" literature. Moreover, the politics of Theory, its one and only center, focused on group resentment, not only lacks leverage in the real world of political negotiation and compromise but blocks a vision of value genuinely transcendent of that world.

The American Right's attack on "permissive" leftist values equally misses the point, which is that the very capitalist culture the Right glorifies promotes the cultural hedonism the Right deplores. On its part, Theory sees capitalism as the barrier to decentered, hedonistic freeplay rather than the ground for it. The decentered self, in practice, adopts a consumerist rather than a revolutionary subject position. Indeed, a vulgar Marxist analysis might suggest that assaults on bourgeois morality *serve the needs* of a dynamic, innovation-driven postmodern market economy. Daniel Bell argues, in "The Cultural Contradictions of Capitalism," that the present sociopolitical order has little to fear from the academic Left but that a reversion to the Protestant ethos of deferred gratification would devastate it (Bell and Kristol, 51).

Bell sees the postmodernist culture that capitalism has produced as a contradiction *within* contemporary capitalism: "The 'new capitalism' . . . continued to demand a Protestant Ethic in the area of production—that is the realm of work—but to stimulate a demand for pleasure and play in the area of consumption" (51). Thus "[the] breakup of the traditional bourgeois economic system, in fact, was brought about by the bourgeois economic system—by the free market to be precise" (50). It is a traditional Marxist practice to undermine capitalism by showing its contradictions but Theory is in no position to do this, having bought into the capitalist system by way of its endorsement of the fragmented Desire *that is precisely the socially constructed form of consumerist psychology.* Thus capitalism has its contradictions, just not the ones Theory supposes.

If Theory did not exist, capitalism would need to invent it. Though critics like Belsey are sincere in their opposition to postmodernist capitalism's power structure, they serve its ends as well as if they were a capitalist Fifth Column infiltrated into the holdout world of the humanities. Theory's assault on the ethical tradition of literary humanism is an instance. The ethically oriented literary critic David Parker notes "the curious paradox . . . that while it is those who claim affiliation with the Left who have most consistently attacked the ethical, the result of such attacks has been to make us more powerless than we might have been in the face of the machinery of late capitalism" (*Ethics, Theory, and the Novel*, 210). Without the ethical resources of the past, "ethical inarticulacy will all too often make us prey to the image-makers, the advertisers, and politicians" (196).

I believe Richard Stivers's *The Culture of Cynicism* to be a compelling account of the ethical inarticulateness of contemporary American culture. Stivers traces how "consumption fragments the individual into multiple selves and roles, each realized in a different commodity" (54). Theory's attack on the integral "bourgeois" self reinforces a socioeconomic order dependent on self-fragmentation: "The more one's self is fragmented, culturally and technologically, the less one is able to resist obeying technical rules—no matter how absurd, no matter how immoral. Only a unified self, a moral self, is capable of placing *specific* rules into a more *general* context" (93). Theory thus expends its energy and anger on beating a dead horse, jettisoning the inner-directed self that could enable a vestigial resistance to the unmediated consumer society: "The inner-directed character occurs in a culture that forms an individual with a conscience, an internalized set of beliefs, that permits, actually requires, one to follow it when no one else is around or in the face of opposition from others" (128), whereas the fragmented self celebrated by Theory is one that "leaves the individual with no moral defenses against the tyranny of the group" (129). Stivers argues that the "universal suspicion and the attack on language" characteristic of Theory lead to hopeless passivity rather than social protest (179). The notion that the denial of connection between sense and referent leads automatically to revolutionary consciousness has it backward. Theory conspires with the fashion in which "modern societies have institutionalized meaninglessness" (175).

Get Real

In opposition to Theory's privileging of fragmentation, I wish to defend a description of a self, neither "bourgeois humanist" nor *totally* circumscribed by race-gender-class; neither fully integrated and self-same nor floating about in the vague inane of Derridean "freeplay." The self I observe in our culture is *struggling* to cohere just enough to have a life, share it with others, get some ethical purchase, and even achieve moments of spiritual revelation. This is not easy. No one has a single, unchanging self whose identity, unalterably and inalienably assigned at birth, passively accrues interest on its original investment until death. Yet a viable self needs to move *toward* coherence and cogency. As Colin Falck says, "Subjectivity must be seen as something we come into, rather than as something which we are equipped with fully-fledged and by definition" (134). Self might be best conceived of not as stable *or* unstable, autonomous *or* socially constructed but as coming into and fading out of focus, of having more real and less real moments.

The philosopher Robert Nozick argues that we are "more real at some times than at others, more real in some modes than in others. . . . Some say during sexual excitement, some say when they are alert and learning new things." Our reality is a work in progress, a project of self-making: "Our identity consists of those features, aspects, and activities that don't just exist but also are (more) real. The greater reality a feature has, the more weight it has in our identity. Our reality consists partly in the values we pursue and live by, the vividness, intensity and integration by which we embody them. . . . In saying that we are constituted by our reality, I mean to say the substance of the self is the reality it manages to achieve" (131–32). For Charles Altieri, "Individuals become selves to the degree that we imagine them caring about the identities they take on" (*Subjective Agency,* 25).

In becoming real, our chance of resisting the unreality that surrounds us becomes more possible. The decentered and disconnected self has much to do with contemporary political apathy. Our commercial culture effectively practices the linguistic evacuation of determinable meaning that Theory preaches, having perfected the separation of signifiers from referents as T. J. Jackson Lears argues is the case with advertising: "Promising relief from feelings of unreality, advertising nevertheless exacerbated those feelings by hastening what . . . Henri Lefebvre has called 'the decline of the referentials'—the tendency, under corporate capitalism, for words to become severed from any meaningful referent. . . . Under capitalism, visual and verbal signs become detached from all traditional associations and meaning in general is eroded" (21). Theory universalizes a historical contingency brought about by consumer culture into an eternal essence of language, thereby representing culture as nature and effectually acting as an agent rather than subverter of capitalist culture. I see no way to respond effectively to the decline of referentials except by remapping the relation of discourse, rhetoric, and representation to experience.

The Assault on Spirit

The most important cultural role of literature today may be to recover spiritual and ethical reality by deepening and intensifying a dispiritingly light and thin literary, cultural, and academic discourse on life as we live it and meaning as we experience it. Fiction centers on persons rather than collectivities, standpoints, subject positions. It discovers the new, gives us the shock of it. It gives us momentary and fragile glimpses, never to be secured, of what deconstructionists dread and misrepresent, that is, the feeling of presence.

It is, after all, mysterious that Theory centers its "politics" on literature. Why literature? My argument has been that it is because the academic Left's political views do not bear direct argument, particularly argument that must consider rather than facilely dismiss other visions of politics. Literature and cultural studies allows the academic Left to ruthlessly criticize everything existing without the embarrassment of having to responsibly argue alternative positions.

In the dubiously named "Evidence" issue of *PMLA* Heather Dubrow asserts that "there's still an imperative to prove—for example, proving the oppression of women in early modern England and *hence* proving current oppression" (29; my emphasis). Of course, the former in no way *proves* the latter. Dubrow mistakes history for essentialist metaphysics—once true, always true—or, perhaps, for propaganda. There *may* be a connection but it is precisely the historical connection that must *be* proven, not be assumed and then presented *as* a proof.

There is politics in literature but Theory never explains convincingly why politics alone should be privileged. The most illuminating political meanings in literature are frequently the least susceptible to the reductions of propaganda. Writers from communist and formerly communist countries understand this clearly, knowing from experience that *the very politicization of everything desired by Theory is a powerful form of oppression.* The society that put the total politicization of all aspects of life and self into practice was the Soviet Union where, as Leszek Kolakowski observes, it was a principle "that every activity—economic, cultural, etc.—must be completely subordinated to the aims of the state; that not only are acts against the regime forbidden and ruthlessly punished but that no political actions are 'neutral' and the individual has no right to do anything that is not part of the state's purposes; that he is the state's property and treated by it as such" (2:514).

One of the most curious outcomes of Theory is that the motive for becoming a university professor of English used to be a love of literature whereas now it seems to a hatred of it. Writers outrage the politically orthodox because they do not echo what we always already know is the righteous view, the correct Theory line. David Parker suggests that what really animates Theory's hatred of the canon is that the canon operates "as subversive Other to the suppressive will of hegemonic Theory" (*Ethics, Theory, and the Novel*, 146). Eugene Goodheart sees art as making dogmatists uneasy: "The province of the artist is precisely one area in which the regime of politics is always insecure; the self, personal desire, and fantasy" (14).

Theory does value women and minority writers on the basis of their ascribed subject positions as reliable spokespersons for oppressed communities. These writers represent the collective truth of their group rather than the oppressive ideology of bourgeois individuality. But minority writers are beginning to protest a sanctification that depends on their reduction to Theory's terms. In an eloquent essay,

Amy Tan protests the grounds of her canonization: "Apparently I am driven to capture the immigrant experience, to demystify Chinese culture, to point out the differences between Chinese and American culture, even to pave the way for other Asian American writers. If only I were that noble" (28).

In a comment that strikes to the heart of the political fallacy in Theory, she observes, "If I knew what to do about immigration, I would be a sociologist or a politician and not a long-winded storyteller." There is a basic misconception of aims: "I write to discover the past for myself. I don't write to change the future for others" (30). Tan's very provisionality gives a reason for readers to take the risk of trust: "Writing, for me, is an act of faith, a hope that I will discover what I mean by 'truth.' I also think of reading as an act of faith, a hope that I will discover something remarkable about ordinary life, about myself. And if the writer and reader discover the same thing, if they have that connection, the act of faith has resulted in an act of magic" (30–31). Tan clearly does not wish to be dehumanized into a display screen for preconceived political dogma.

Theory's assault on literature is part of a more general assault on spirit. In 1986 Jonathan Culler called upon comparative literature professors to engage in a search-and-destroy mission against the religious beliefs of their students. This was "because religion provides an ideological legitimation for many reactionary or repressive forces in American society today" (30–32). Culler was reacting to the . religious right, the "moral majority." But to so generalize his attack he needed to repress the historical memory of the crucial engagement of Protestant ministers, black and white, and Catholic priests and nuns in the Civil Rights movement of the 1960s. Stivers notes how, in postmodern culture, sensationally immediate images become a substitute for memory that "is tied to a remembrance of the past, of what is significant in the past" (143). Stephen Carter, questioning the academic leftist denigration of religion as always allied to political oppression, cites the February 1956 letter by Joseph Rummel, the Archbishop of New Orleans, that declared segregation a sin, followed up by his editorial in a church publication warning Catholic legislators that any vote supporting segregation would result in "'automatic excommunication'" (63). Of course, Culler's hostility was always already inscribed by his academic community. His essay is historically amnesiac.

Culler calls for "a vigorous tradition of antireligious satire to keep the sanc-timonious in check" (31). Keeping the sanctimonious in check is fine, but the problem is that within the context of his own community of Theory it is his voice that is sanctimonious and his project would work to silence students rather than to liberate them. Carter notes that "for all the calls for diversity in the hiring of university faculty, one rarely hears such arguments in favor of the devoutly religious—a group, according to survey data, that is grossly underrepresented on campus" (57). Since blacks are higher than most other groups in church attendance and membership, and tend toward fundamentalist or conservative religious views, it is questionable how well they are "represented" by "progressive" black faculty (60). Of course, Theory believes that religion is part of what blacks need liberating from, a justification rather like that which used to be made for the civilizing mission of colonialism.

In fact, Theory's hostility to Judaic and Christian religion is an inheritance from Marxism, which became, in effect, a competing religion. And so with Theory, which functions for the academic Left as a *kind* of religion, offering dogma, verbal rituals (jargon), and a community of belief. Theory, like Marxism, hates religious discourse as a *competitive* vision.

John Gray argues the religious structure of Marxist belief: "The attraction of Marxism to the Western intelligentsia was . . . never that of an analytically superior theoretical system in social science. It was rather the appeal of a historical theodicy, in which Judeo-Christian moral hopes were to be realized without the need for a transcendental commitment" (83). Peter Berger defines the ideology of Theory as "a secular theodicy. The term 'theodicy' is to be understood in the sense given it by Max Weber: any coherent explanation of evil and suffering" ("World View," 51). Comparison seems in order: Does Theory give the most coherent explanation of evil and suffering? Ernest Gellner saw the central flaw in Marxism to be a blindness to existential exigency: "Marxism does promise a total salvation, but not to individuals, only to mankind as a totality. It has virtually nothing to say to an individual in personal anguish or in some kind of life crisis. . . . Marxism has nothing to say to personal tragedy and bereavement" (39–40). As we have seen throughout, Theory follows Marxism in its interest not in selves and their suffering or joy but in categorical groups, whose oppression it appropriates. Certainly it touches on real injustice and suffering, but injustice, though it may originate in hatred of a group, can only be suffered person by person.

Theory has no language for suffering or *any other feeling* that is not related to its prescribed categories. The category of person being *proscribed*, pain and loss are reduced to a text. Edward Mendelson recalls: "Some years ago a senior member of the Textualist International referred in a lecture to 'wars and other texts.' One of his colleagues replied, 'Yes, my father died in one of those texts'" (63). It cheapens anguish to reduce it into a solely political category and to use it as a commodity, trying to corner the market in it while dismissing or demeaning unauthorized forms of it.

So, too, for alienation. In religion, alienation is the separation of the self from God, a non-Marxist secularized version of which would be Meaning. It is manifested in feelings of metaphysical homelessness, lostness, and emptiness, and its greatest philosophical expositor is not Feuerbach or Marx but Kierkegaard, who saw it as the dark night of the soul that *evidenced* the reality of spirit. Kierkegaard demonstrated, as had Pascal, that those who do not experience alienation in its psychological and spiritual form merely repress it rather than free themselves from it. They evade spiritual authenticity either passively by various opiates or actively by self-magnifying projects. Marx famously termed religion "the opium of the people," a diversion from the "real," that is, political, cause of their alienation. But it may be that it is Marxism that has become *The Opium of the Intellectuals*, to echo the title of Raymond Aron's book on the irresponsibility of the postwar French Left. Donald Barthelme quipped: "The new opium of the people is opium, or at least morphine. In a situation in which morphine contends with morpheme, the latter loses every time" (50).

True, as I noted for Derrida and Foucault in chapter 1, Theory has lately backed off from some of its negations. Moreover, it has even engaged in a belated attempt to embrace ethics. Sean Burke's *The Death and Return of the Author* demonstrates how major theorists quietly dropped their cancellations of selfhood, while David Parker's 1991 essay noted even in Theory the return of the repressed of ethical valuation ("Evaluative Discourse and the Return of the Repressed"). But besides that the camp followers of Theory still recite its obsolete negative dogma as leading-edge high-tech criticism, Theory simply carries too much baggage to function as a credible ethical discourse. When Theory talks ethics, it is as if it is celebrating itself for having rediscovered the wheel.

A Spiritual Interrogation of Theory

Theory's privileging of political discourse over ethical, literary, and theological discourse may be reversed so as to interpret Theory's politics by way of theology and ethics.

A number of critics have observed how Theory rejects any limitation on the power of Theory or Theorist. This lust for power bleeds over from Theory's discursive Godfather, Marxism. Daniel Bell argues that Marxism reflects "the megalomania of self-infinitization" (Bell and Kristol, 42). Joel Whitebook sees it as infantile:

> Infantilism involves an enormous sense of grandiosity and fantasies of omnicompetence. . . . What maturity has to offer in recompense for the abandoned desires of grandiosity is the satisfaction of dignity, autonomy, and mutual recognition. It cannot be denied however, that the grandiose disavowal of finitude—death, suffering and lack—cannot be compensated. In this respect, maturity is relatively austere and completely disconsolate. (165)

What Theory does offer is Marx's megalomaniac project to attack everything that exists, a project shared by Foucault. If, as Frank Palmer defines it, moral discourse is grounded in "a sense of one's own finitude in a world which existed before we were born and will remain after we die" (149), Theory lacks such grounding. Theory negates dignity, autonomy, and any *mutuality* of recognition. Steven Watts indicts "the brittle narcissism of poststructuralism," notes "its self-gratifying, narrowly intellectualist, and illusory understanding of ideas and culture, politics and power" and concludes that "the linguistic Left has encouraged not so much illumination and liberation, but rather hubris and self-delusion" (633). If these critics are right, a pathological resentment at existence per se underwrites Theory.

Foucault and Althusser are exemplary for this case. Foucault's obsession with power is apparent in an interview where he explains his rejection of humanism:

> By humanism I mean the totality of discourse through which Western man is told: "Even though you don't exercise power, you can still be a ruler. Better yet, the more you deny yourself the exercise of power, the more you submit to those in power, then the more this increases your sovereignty." Humanism invented a whole series of subjected sovereignties: the soul (ruling the body, but subjected to God), consciousness (sovereign in a context of judgment, but subjected to the necessities of truth), the individual (a titular control of personal rights subjected to the laws of nature and society), basic freedom (sovereign within, but accepting the demands of an outside world and "aligned with destiny"). In short, humanism is everything in Western civilization that restricts *the desire for power*: it prohibits the desire for power and excludes the possibility of power being seized. (*Language, Counter-Memory, Practice*, 221–22)

Foucault's history is, as always, dubious, since the evidence is that the humanism of the Renaissance and eighteenth century vastly increased and democratized power, at least in comparison with any earlier politico-economic formation or with socialist revolutionary formations later. One could argue that this increase in power was spiritually damaging, but Foucault argues against any *limitation* on the desire for power. This is a spiritually pathological vision, and it is no wonder that Foucault and his followers detest not only realities but reality, rejecting moral personhood, society, the outside world, nature. This infantile megalomania may reject the self but makes grandiose claims for an absolute egoistic solipsism.

Foucault's theory of discourse is clarified in this context. If everything is discourse, he can control it in his mind and change "reality" by redescribing it. Others, who might resist redefinition, are airbrushed out by Foucault's sweeping denial of subjectivity and authorial agency. One working result of Theory is to enable solipsism. In the academy, Foucault came very near to sweeping the field of any discourse but Foucaldeanism.

Althusser's is an even more obvious and far sadder case. In his autobiography, *The Future Lasts Forever*, he "explains" (and exculpates) his life entirely in psychological rather than political terms. His problems were that he never felt quite real, even physically: "My body felt a deep-seated desire to achieve its own existence" (213). The desire to feel more real led him "to invest and inscribe [his] objective, public activities with [his] subjective phantasies" (160). Vicariously identifying with an idealized stereotype of a working class reflected his "desire to become involved in *the real world,* with all sorts of people, and the desire above all to fraternise with the most deprived, the most straightforward, the purest, and the most honest" (200; my emphasis). Skepticism about the supposedly bourgeois concept, "reality," here vanishes in a mist of primitivist sentimentality.

Althusser's attitudes toward gender are interesting in the light of the politically correct standards to which his disciples hold canonical writers. He blames his feelings of insubstantiality and his dissociation from his body on a castrating mother (138). He found it necessary always to keep "a reserve of women" to supplement his wife because of a fear of loneliness (106). He explains his strangling of his wife as a sort of favor to her, accepting his psychologist's discursive formulation of it as an "'altruistic suicide'" (281): "The fact is I strangled my wife, who meant everything to me, during an intense and unforeseeable state of mental confusion. . . . She loved me so much, and since she could not go on living, she wanted to die. Unaware of what I was doing and in a state of confusion, I must have 'done what she wanted,' which she did not resist and which caused her death" (3). I will not argue against Althusser's explanation, but I do ask the reader to imagine how progressives would respond to the same "discourse" coming from a conservative academic in the same circumstances.

Althusser appeals to an objectivity often denied in his name: "People will, of course, believe me when I say my intention is to be as *objective* as humanly possible" (28). He declares the validity of his work to be entirely unrelated to his life: "Whatever a philosopher's conscious or unconscious inner motivations might be, his published philosophy has an entirely *objective reality* and its effects on the world if it has one is similarly *objective* and may, thank God, have almost no connection with the inner world I have described. Philosophy, like every other activity come to that, is nothing more than the pure interiority of all the subjectivities in the world, each enclosed in its own solipsism" (175). How can purely interior solipsism attain "entirely *objective reality*"?

But even if we were to concede Althusser's argument, why should we privilege a philosophy that has no connection with our inner world as the master key to the literature that traces the complications of just that inner world? If Althusser's discourse is exempted from suspicion, on what grounds do progressives trash canonical writers for having fallen short of the political perfection of 2003? Is the personal somehow not the political in just this one instance? If Althusser's philosophy has no relation whatsoever to the existential exigencies of *his* life, how can it be used to explain everything that matters about *ours*?

Certainly Althusser's confession is at the least an extraordinary compendium of bad faith; is not this bad faith allowed for by his rejection of "bourgeois moral-ity"? Dietrich Bonhoeffer, Lutheran minister, influence on liberation theology, hanged by the Nazis in 1943 after having returned to Germany to assist in the Resistance, brings home the need to have a notion of truth and reality not depen-dent on ideological convenience: "There is a truth which is of Satan. Its essence is that under the semblance of truth it denies everything that is real. It lives upon hatred of the real and of the world. . . . God's truth judges created things out of love, and Satan's truth judges them out of envy and hatred. God's truth has become flesh in the world and is alive in the real, but Satan's truth is the death of all reality" (cited in Bok, 304).

Ideological state apparatuses do come into Althusser's narrative at one point: He complains of the obvious unfairness of the accusation that he was "protected by the educational Ideological State Apparatus of which I was a member." This is a "witch hunt" (*The Future Lasts Forever*, 256–57). His rather brief confinement in an asylum did alert him to another injustice: "What can now be done to free the mentally ill from the Hell created for them by the combined operations of all the Ideological State Apparatuses?" (274).

Finally, he offers another explanation of the killing, one that convincingly accords with his solipsistic spiritual dilemma: killing his wife was just part of an attempt to destroy any evidence of his own existence: "The best way of proving you do not exist is to destroy yourself by destroying the person who loves you and above all believes in your *existence*" (278, 283). Thus Althusser himself tellingly relates his killing of his wife *to the fear and hatred of reality his entire corpus of writings inscribes*. Althusser does seem to have had an agonizingly decentered self, and this spiritual and psychological disorder seems to have had everything to do with his life and with his thought.

There are, then, grounds to speculate that Theory's problems with reality and transcendence extend from the political to the psychological, spiritual, and metaphysical. Theory's project in this light attains some coherence. It is only natural that those who have a "self-destructive dream of an existence without boundaries" (Goodheart, 19) will resent reality and realism, especially at their most quotidian. This accounts for the peculiarly undifferentiated and totalistic quality of Foucauldian and Althusserian rejection.

In contrast to the infantile egoism of Theory, the literary work inspires an activity not only intertextual but interpersonal, a form where minds, feelings, and spirits connect in engagement, whether or not in agreement. A number of ethically centered culture and literary critics converge on this insight, among them Frank Palmer, David Parker, Martha Nussbaum, Wayne Booth, William E. Cain, Peter Dews, Colin Falck, Richard Stivers, Sissela Bok, Judith Shklar, and the novelist and philosopher Iris Murdoch. Wolfgang Iser, Richard Freadman, and Rita Felski

(*Beyond Feminist Aesthetics*) show how the ethical relations of author, novel, and reader expand the moral possibilities of the much maligned realist novel. In my view, one encounters in any of these critical thinkers a more sophisticated and credible moral perspective than in the collected oeuvre of Theory.

Frank Palmer puts clearly what Theory denies: "Part of the value we find in literature consists in our negotiation with a human mind other than our own" (159). Theory's idealist and solipsistic tendencies are as oppositional to literary discovery as they are to ethical or political inquiry. Supposedly this is for the sake of liberation, but solipsistic liberation is something of an oxymoron. In the ethical philosopher Judith Shklar's eloquent formulation, the unjust citizen is "morally deaf and dissociated" (48). Francis Jacques finely describes the wicked man as "swamped and lost in himself" (98). Virtue, as Iris Murdoch comprehends it, "is concerned with really apprehending that other people exist" ("The Sublime and the Beautiful Revisited," 270). This holds for homosexual and heterosexual relations alike but cannot hold for relations entirely abstracted into ascribed political group meanings.

Outside Theory, in the real world, readers not only form relationships with literary works but discover possibilities for richer human relationships inscribed within them. Far from the canon entombing a set of static values, it *consists* of works that show a capacity to be infinitely renewed, reread, Faulkner *and* Toni Morrison. Parker's defense of the centrality of ethics to literature does not deny the social constructedness of our feelings and responses: "We learn, largely from our culture, how to feel or when to emote" (99). But there are better and worse ways of learning and feeling, with the worst of all proceeding from a wholly theoretical and negative conception of the self. How works become and remain classic is in relation to their capacity for conveying richer and more complex possibilities of feeling. Of course, this view requires the reinstatement of the denied category of experience.

Peter Berger argues that the case for transcendence lies not beyond but in the structure of our experience, the experience of *"an other reality, . . .* one of ultimate significance for man, which transcends the reality within which our everyday experience unfolds" (*Rumor of Angels*, 2). Berger, with Thomas Luckmann, was author of a major influence on Theory, the 1966 book *The Social Construction of Reality*. Theory, however, has attempted to disappear Berger since his 1970 book, *A Rumor of Angels: Modern Society and the Rediscovery of the Supernatural*, in which he argues that although beliefs are socially constructed for the most part, "it is possible to liberate oneself to a considerable degree from the taken-for-granted assumptions of one's own time" (27), and he cites academically unfashionable religious belief as an example.

Berger fully recognizes that in the hegemonic interpretive community of the University his religious beliefs constitute him as other, a member of a "cognitive minority," that is, "a group of people whose view of the world differs significantly from the one generally taken for granted in their society" (6). In Theory jargon,

he is "different," "other." In common with those who challenge hegemony in whatever form, he must rely on his perceptions rather than his community's theory of
them. Doing so, he suggests that we seriously attend to "signals of transcendence":
"phenomena that are to be found within the domain of our 'natural' reality but that
appear to point beyond that reality" (52–53). As he notes, "Human life gains the
greatest part of its richness from the capacity for ecstasy, by which I do not mean
the alleged experiences of the mystic, but any experience of stepping outside the
taken-for-granted reality of everyday life, any openness to the mystery that surrounds us on all sides. A philosophical anthropology worthy of the name will have
to regain a perception of these experiences, and with this regain a metaphysical
dimension" (75).

These realizations can be inductively derived "from generally accepted experience" (76). In religious discourse it is again a question not of dogmatic authority
but of "*What is being said here? What is the human experience out of which these sayings came?
And then: To what extent, and in what way, may we see here genuine discoveries of transcendent
truth?*" (84). So stated, it is difficult to see what disproof of Berger's argument could
be consistent with Theory's own professions of absolute faith in the "things which
are not seen" of Theory over perceived reality.

St. Paul preached that "we look not at the things which are seen, but at the
things which are not seen; for the things which are seen are temporal, but the
things which are not seen are eternal" (2 Corinthians 4:18). Poets give glimpses of
things that are not seen through things that are, pointing to what lies just beyond
our quotidian horizon of perception in certain privileged moments:

> the moment in the rose garden,
> The moment in the arbour where the rain beat,
> The moment in the draughty church at smokefall.
> (Eliot, "Four Quartets," 119–20)

So far as discourses of oppression go, there is more ethical resonance in "I do
not know. Am I my brother's keeper?" and "The voice of your brother's blood cries
out from the ground" than in the collected works of Foucault. The language is more
real and the facts of the matter more authentic. If discourse creates reality, is it not
then essential that our education include "images of high humanity with which the
pupil of whatever class might identify" (Nussbaum, 205). Ihab Hassan confesses
that "on some days—they are rare—I suspect that literature touches the *mysterium
tremendum et fascinans*," noting the tendency of contemporary critical discourse to
"become surly before those incandescent moments that pervade literature. We
have no will, certainly no idiom, to attest sudden, radical breaks with the ordinary
world" (119).

Theory fears encountering these incandescent moments without always already knowing and discounting them, a certitude that the dogmas of Theory provide. Theory protects the self-isolated ego from otherness, surprise, reality, and transcendence, responding to what Murdoch sees as the pathology of solipsistic idealism, "a fear of contingency, a yearning to pierce through the messy phenomenal world to some perfect and necessary form and order" ("Sublime and the Beautiful Revisited," 259–60). Theory constitutes that safe and airless ideal realm.

Works Cited

Abrams, Meyer Herbert. "What Is a Humanistic Criticism?" In Dwight Eddins, ed., *The Emperor Redressed*, 13–44. Tuscaloosa: University of Alabama Press, 1995.

Althusser, Louis. *Lenin and Philosophy and Other Essays*. Translated by Ben Brewster. New York: Monthly Review Press, 1971.

———. *The Future Lasts Forever*. Translated by Richard Veasey. New York: New Press, 1992.

Altieri, Charles. *Canons and Consequences*. Evanston: Northwestern University Press, 1990.

———. *Subjective Agency*. Oxford: Blackwell, 1994.

Appiah, Anthony. *In My Father's House*. Oxford: Oxford University Press, 1992.

Aron, Raymond. *The Opium of the Intellectuals*. Translated by Terence Kilmartin. London: Secker and Warburg, 1957.

Bakhtin, Mikhail Mikhailovich. *The Dialogic Imagination*. Edited by Michael Holquist. Translated by Caryl Emerson and Michael Holquist. Austin: University of Texas Press, 1981.

Barthelme, Donald. "Donald Barthelme." Interview with Jerome Klinkowitz. In Joe David Bellamy, ed., *The New Fiction*, 45–54. Urbana: University of Illinois Press, 1974.

Barthes, Roland. *Mythologies*. Translated by Annette Lavers. New York: Farrar, Straus, and Giroux, 1972.

———. *S/Z*. Translated by Richard Miller. New York: Farrar, Straus, and Giroux, 1974.

Bauer, Dale. "The Other 'F' Word: Feminist in the Classroom." *College English* 52 (1990): 385–96.

———. "Dale M. Bauer Responds." *College English* 53, no. 1 (1991): 103–4.

———. "Gender in Bakhtin's Carnival." In Robyn R. Warhol and Diane Price Herndl, eds., *Feminisms*, 671–84. New Brunswick, N.J.: Rutgers University Press, 1991.

———. *Edith Wharton's Brave New World*. Madison: University of Wisconsin Press, 1994.

Baym, Nina. "The Madwoman and Her Languages: Why I Don't Do Feminist Literary Theory." In Robyn R. Warhol and Diane Price Herndl, eds., *Feminisms*, 154–67. New Brunswick, N.J.: Rutgers University Press, 1991.

———. "The Agony of Feminism: Why Feminist Theory Is Necessary After All."

In Dwight Eddins, ed., 101–17. *The Emperor Redressed*. Tuscaloosa: University of Alabama Press, 1995.

Becker, Jasper. *Hungry Ghosts*. London: John Murray, 1996.

Bell, Daniel. *The Cultural Contradictions of Capitalism*. New York: Basic Books, 1976.

Bell, Daniel, and Irving Kristol, eds. *Capitalism Today*. New York: New American Library, 1971.

Bell, Michael Davitt. *The Development of American Romance: The Sacrifice of Relation*. Chicago: Chicago University Press, 1980.

Belsey, Catherine. *Critical Practice*. London: Methuen, 1980.

———. "Constructing the Subject: Deconstructing the Text." In Robyn R. Warhol and Diane Price Herndl, eds., *Feminisms*, 593–609. New Brunswick, N.J.: Rutgers University Press, 1991.

Benton, Ted. *The Rise and Fall of Structural Marxism*. London: Macmillan, 1994.

Bercovitch, Sacvan. *The American Jeremiad*. Madison: University of Wisconsin Press, 1978.

———. "The Problem of Ideology in American Literary History." *Critical Inquiry* 12, no. 4 (1986): 631–53.

Berger, Brigitte. "Muticulturalism and the Modern University." *Partisan Review* 60, no. 4 (1993): 516–26.

Berger, Peter L. *A Rumor of Angels: Modern Society and the Recovery of the Supernatural*. Garden City, N.Y.: Doubleday, 1970.

———. "The World View of the New Class: Secularity and Its Discontents." In B. Bruce-Biggs, ed., *The New Class?* 49–55. New Brunswick, N.J.: Transaction, 1979.

———. *The Capitalist Revolution: Fifty Propositions about Prosperity, Equality, and Liberty*. New York: Basic Books, 1986.

Berman, Paul, ed. *Debating P. C.* New York: Dell, 1992.

Berreby, David. "That Damned Elusive Bruno Latour." *Lingua Franca* (October 1994): 22–32, 78.

Bok, Sissela. *Lying*. New York: Vintage, 1979.

Bové, Paul A. "Discourse." In Frank Lentricchia and Thomas McLaughlin, eds., *Critical Terms for Literary Study*, 50–65. Chicago: University of Chicago Press, 1995.

Bredin, Hugh. "The Displacement of Character in Narrative Theory." *British Journal of Aesthetics* 22 (1982): 291–99.

Brodhead, Richard. "Sparing the Rod: Discipline and Fiction in Antebellum America." In Philip Fisher, ed., *The New American Studies*, 141–70. Berkeley: University of California Press, 1991.

Bruce-Biggs, B., ed. *The New Class?* New Brunswick, N.J.: Transaction, 1979.

Burke, Sean. *The Death and Return of the Author*. Edinburgh: Edinburgh University Press, 1992.

Caesar, Terry. *Conspiring with Forms.* Athens: University of Georgia Press, 1992.

Carter, Stephen L. *The Culture of Disbelief.* New York: Basic Books, 1993.

Clayton, Jay. *The Pleasures of Babel.* New York: Oxford University Press, 1993.

Coulson, Jessie, H. W. Fowler, and William Little, joint authors. C. T. Onions, ed. *The Shorter Oxford English Dictionary on Historical Principles.* Third edition. Oxford: Oxford University Press, 1967.

Culler, Jonathan. "Comparative Literature and the Pieties." *Profession* 86 (1986): 30–32.

D'Emilio, John. "Capitalism and Gay Identity." In Ann Snitow, Christine Tansell, and Sharon Thompson, eds., *Powers of Desire,* 100–13. New York: Monthly Review Press, 1983.

Denning, Michael. "'The Special American Conditions': Marxism and American Studies." *American Quarterly* 38, no. 3 (1986): 356–80.

Derrida, Jacques. "Structure, Sign, and Play in the Discourse of the Humanities." In Eugene Donato and Richard Macksey, eds., *The Structuralist Controversy.* Baltimore: The Johns Hopkins University Press, 1972: 247–72.

———. *Of Grammatology.* Translated by Gayatri Chakravorty Spivak. Baltimore: The Johns Hopkins University Press, 1976.

———. *Limited Incorporated.* Baltimore: The Johns Hopkins University Press, 1977.

———. "Like the Sound of the Deep Sea within a Shell." *Critical Inquiry* 15, no. 4 (summer 1989): 590–652.

———. *Deconstruction in a Nutshell.* Edited by John Caputo. New York: Fordham University Press, 1997.

Dews, Peter. *Logics of Discrimination.* London: Verso, 1987.

Donato, Eugene, and Richard Macksey, eds. *The Structuralist Controversy.* Baltimore: The Johns Hopkins University Press, 1972.

Dryden, Edgar. *Melville's Thematics of Form.* Baltimore: The Johns Hopkins University Press, 1981.

Dubrow, Heather. Introduction to "The Status of Evidence." *PMLA* 111, no. 1 (1996): 7–20.

———. "The Status of Evidence: A Roundtable." *PMLA* 111, no. 1 (1996): 21–31.

Eagleton, Terry. *The Illusions of Postmodernism.* Oxford: Blackwell, 1996.

Easterlin, Nancy, and Barbara Riebling, eds. *After Poststructuralism.* Evanston: Northwestern University Press, 1993.

Easthope, Anthony. *British Post-Structuralism since 1968.* London: Routlege, 1988.

Easton, Lloyd D., and Kurt H. Guddat. Introduction to *Writings of the Young Marx on Philosophy and Society.* Edited and translated by Lloyd D. Easton and Kurt H. Guddat. Garden City, N.Y.: Doubleday Anchor, 1967.

Echols, Alice. "The Taming of the Id: Feminist Sexual Politics, 1968–83." In Carole S. Vance, ed., *Pleasure and Danger,* 138–49. Boston: Routledge and Kegan Paul, 1984.

Eddins, Dwight, ed. *The Emperor Redressed*. Tuscaloosa: University of Alabama Press, 1995.

Eliot, George. *Middlemarch*. Norton Critical Edition. New York: W. W. Norton, 1977.

Eliot, T. S. *The Complete Poems and Plays, 1909–1950*. New York: Harcourt, Brace, and World, 1971.

Elshtain, Joan Bethke. *Democracy on Trial*. New York: Basic Books, 1995.

Elster, Jon. *An Introduction to Karl Marx*. Cambridge: Cambridge University Press, 1986.

Falck, Colin. *Myth, Truth, and Literature*. Cambridge: Cambridge University Press, 1994.

Falcoff, Mark. "North of the Border." *TLS*, March 17, 1996, 15.

Felski, Rita. *Beyond Feminist Aesthetics*. Cambridge, Mass.: Harvard University Press, 1989.

———. "Feminism, Postmodernism, and the Critique of Modernity." *Cultural Critique* 13 (1989): 33–56.

Feuerbach, Ludwig. *The Essence of Christianity*. 1841. Translated by George Eliot. New York: Harper and Row, 1957.

Fish, Stanley. "Rhetoric." In Frank Lentricchia and Thomas McLaughlin, eds., *Critical Terms for Literary Study*, 203–22. Chicago: University of Chicago Press, 1995.

Foucault, Michel. *The Archeology of Knowledge*. Translated by A. M. Sheridan Smith. New York: Pantheon, 1972.

———. *The Order of Things*. New York: Vintage, 1973.

———. *Madness and Civilization*. Translated by Richard Howard. New York: Vintage, 1973.

———. *Language, Counter-Memory, Practice*. Translated by Donald F. Bouchard and Sherry Simon. Ithaca: Cornell University Press, 1977.

———. *Discipline and Punish*. Translated by Alan Sheridan. New York: Pantheon 1977.

———. "What Is an Author?" In Josué V. Harari, ed., *Textual Strategies*. Ithaca: Cornell University Press, 1979: 141–60.

———. *Power/Knowledge*. Edited by Colin Gordon. Translated by Leo Marshall Gordon, John Mepham, and Kate Soper. New York: Pantheon, 1980.

———. "An Exchange with Michel Foucault." *New York Review of Books*, March 31, 1983, 42.

Fox, Richard Wightman, and T. J. Jackson Lears, eds. *The Culture of Consumption*. New York: Pantheon, 1983.

Fox-Genovese, Elizabeth. *Feminism without Illusions*. Chapel Hill: University of North Carolina Press, 1991.

Freadman, Richard. *Eliot, James, and the Fictional Self: A Study in Character and Narration.* Basingstoke: Macmillan, 1986.

Freadman, Richard, and Seamas Miller. *Re-Thinking Theory.* Cambridge: Cambridge University Press, 1992.

Gallagher, David. "Circe in Uniform." Review of G. Cabrera Infante, *Mea Cuba. TLS,* December 30, 1994, 7.

Gates, Henry Louis, Jr. "'Authenticity' or the Lesson of Little Tree." *New York Times Book Review,* November 24, 1991, 1, 26–30.

Gellner, Ernest. *Conditions of Liberty.* London: Hamish Hamilton, 1994.

Goodheart, Eugene. *Desire and Its Discontents.* New York: Columbia University Press, 1991.

Gouldner, Alvin W. *Against Fragmentation.* New York: Oxford University Press, 1985.

Graff, Gerald. "Co-optation." In H. Aram Veeser, ed., *The New Historicism,* 168–81. London: Routledge, 1989.

Gray, John. *Post-Liberalism.* London: Routledge, 1993.

Green, Renée. "Trading on the Margin." *Transition* 52 (1991): 124–32.

Greenblatt, Stephen. "Towards a Poetics of Culture." In H. Aram Veeser, ed., *The New Historicism,* 1–14. London: Routledge, 1989.

Greene, Jack P. *Pursuits of Happiness.* Chapel Hill: University of North Carolina Press, 1988.

———. *The Intellectual Construction of America: Exceptionalism and Identity from 1492 to 1800.* Chapel Hill: University of North Carolina Press, 1993.

Hall, Stuart, and Tony Jefferson. *Resistance Through Rituals: Youth Subculture in Post-War Britain.* London: Routledge, 1993.

Hamilton, Paul. "On the Verbal Battlefield." *TLS,* September 20, 1985, 1037.

Hamilton, Richard. *The Social Misconstruction of Reality.* New Haven: Yale University Press, 1996.

Harari, Josué V., ed. *Textual Strategies.* Ithaca: Cornell University Press, 1979.

Harding, Nancy. "The Instability of the Analytic Categories of Feminist Theory." *Signs* 11, no. 4 (1986): 645–64.

———. *The Science Question in Feminism.* Ithaca: Cornell University Press, 1986.

———. "Feminism, Science, and the Anti-Enlightenment Critiques." In Linda Nicholson, ed., *Feminism/Postmodernism,* 83–106. New York: Routledge, 1990.

Harper, Philip Brian. *Framing the Margins.* Oxford University Press, 1994.

Hartman, Joan E., and Ellen Messer-Davidow. "Introduction: A Position Statement." In Joan Hartman and Ellen Messer-Davidow, *Engendering Knowledge: Feminists in Academe.* Knoxville: University of Tennessee Press, 1991: 1–7.

Hartsock, Nancy. "The Feminist Standpoint." In Linda Nicholson, ed., *Feminism/Postmodernism,* 216–40. New York: Routledge, 1997.

Hassan, Ihab. "Confessions of a Reluctant Critic; or, The Resistance to Literature."

In Dwight Eddins, ed., *The Emperor Redressed,* 118–31. Tuscaloosa: University of Alabama Press, 1995.

Herbert, Bob. "China's Missing Girls." *New York Times,* October 30, 1997, A23.

Hutner, Gordon, ed. *The American Literary History Reader.* New York: Oxford University Press, 1995.

Iser, Wolfgang. *The Implied Reader.* Baltimore: The Johns Hopkins University Press, 1974.

Jackson, Leonard. *The Poverty of Structuralism.* London: Longman, 1991.

———. *The Dematerialisation of Karl Marx.* London: Longman, 1994.

Jacques, Francis. *Difference and Subjectivity.* Translated by Andrew Rothwell. New Haven: Yale University Press, 1991.

Jameson, Frederic. *The Political Unconscious.* Ithaca: Cornell University Press, 1981.

———. *Postmodernism, or, The Cultural Logic of Late Capitalism.* Durham: Duke University Press, 1991.

———. *The Seeds of Time.* New York: Columbia University Press, 1994.

Johnson, Barbara. "Writing." In Frank Lentricchia and Thomas McLaughlin, eds., *Critical Terms for Literary Study,* 39–49. Chicago: University of Chicago Press, 1995.

Kennedy, Deborah. "A Comment on the 'F' Word: The Feminist in the Classroom." *College English* 53, no. 1 (1991): 101–3.

Khilnani, Sunil. *Arguing Revolution: The Intellectual Left in Postwar France.* New Haven: Yale University Press, 1993.

King, David. *The Commisar Vanishes: The Falsification of Photographs and Art in Stalin's Russia.* New York: Metropolitan Books, 1997.

Kinzer, Stephen. "Muynak Journal: Only Water, Maybe, But It Was a People's Life Blood." *New York Times,* October 28, 1997, 4.

Kolakowski, Leszek. *Main Currents of Marxism.* 3 vols. Translated by P. S. Falla. Oxford: Oxford University Press, 1978.

Kristof, Nicholas D. "Across Asia a Pollution Disaster Hovers." *New York Times,* November 28, 1997, 1.

Kundera, Milan. *The Book of Laughter and Forgetting.* Translated by Michael Henry Heim. Harmondsworth: Penguin, 1981.

———. *Immortality.* Translated by Peter Kussi. New York: Grove Weidenfeld, 1991.

Langer, Elinor. Review of Katherine Frank, *A Voyage Out: The Life of Mary Kingsley. New York Times Book Review,* November 30, 1986, 28.

Lanser, Susan S. "Feminist Criticism, 'The Yellow Wallpaper,' and the Politics of Color in America." *Feminist Studies* 15, no. 3 (1989): 415–51.

Lears, T. J. Jackson. "From Salvation to Self-Realization: Advertising and the Therapeutic Roots of the Consumer Culture." In Richard Wightman Fox and T. J. Jackson Lears, eds., *The Culture of Consumption,* 1–38. New York: Pantheon, 1983.

Lentricchia, Frank. "Last Will and Testament of an Ex-Literary Critic." *Lingua Franca* (September/October 1996): 59–67.

Lentricchia, Frank, and Thomas McLaughlin, eds. *Critical Terms for Literary Study.* Chicago: University of Chicago Press, 1995.

Link, Perry. Review of Vaclav Smil, *China's Ecological Crisis. TLS,* September 10, 1993, 6–7.

———. "Someone Else." *TLS,* October 28, 1994, 8.

Lipset, Seymour Martin. *Continental Divide: The Values and Institutions of the United States and Canada.* Washington, D.C.: Canadian-American Committee, 1989.

Macdonald, Margaret. "The Language of Fiction." In James L. Calderwood and Harold E. Toliver, eds., *Perspectives on Fiction,* 55–70. New York: Oxford University Press, 1968.

Macherey, Pierre. *A Theory of Literary Production.* Translated by Geoffrey Wall. London: Routledge and Kegan Paul, 1978.

Maier, Pauline. "A Marketplace of Human Souls." *New York Times Book Review* (September 5, 1993): 9–10.

Malia, Martin. "The Lesser Evil?" Review essay on Stéphane Courtois, *Le Livre Noir du Communisme.* In *TLS,* March 27, 1998, 3–4.

Marx, Karl. *Capital.* Translated by Samuel Moore and Edward Aveling. New York: Modern Library, 1906.

———. "For a Ruthless Criticism of Everything Existing." Letter to Arnold Ruge, 1843. In David McLellan, ed., *Karl Marx: Selected Writings.* Oxford: Oxford University Press, 1977, 12–15.

———. *Writings of the Young Marx on Philosophy and Society.* Edited and translated by Lloyd D. Easton and Kurt H. Guddat. Garden City, N.Y.: Doubleday Anchor, 1967.

Marx, Karl, and Friedrich Engels. *The German Ideology.* New York: International, 1970.

———. *Basic Writings on Politics and Philosophy.* Edited by Lewis Feuer. Garden City, N.Y.: Doubleday Anchor, 1959.

Mathy, Jean-Philippe. *Extreme Occident: French Intellectuals in America.* Chicago: University of Chicago Press, 1993.

McGowan, John. *Postmodernism and Its Critics.* Ithaca: Cornell University Press, 1991.

Mendelson, Edward. "Caught in the Web of Words." *TLS,* January 16, 1987, 63.

Merquior, José Guilherme. *Foucault.* London: Fontana, 1991.

Messer-Davidow, Ellen. "The Philosophical Bases of Feminist Criticism." *New Literary History* 19, no. 1 (1987): 63–103.

Messer-Davidow, Ellen, and Jane Hartman. "Introduction: A Position Statement." In Jane Hartman and Ellen Messer-Davidow, eds., *Engendering Knowledge: Feminists in Academe,* 1–7. Knoxville: University of Tennessee Press, 1991.

Michaels, Marguerite. "Anne Tyler, Writer 8:05 to 5:30." In Alice Hall Petry, ed., *Critical Essays on Anne Tyler*, 40–44. New York: G. K. Hall, 1992.

Midelfort, H. C. Eric. "Madness and Civilization in Early Modern Europe: A Reappraisal of Michel Foucault." In Barbara C. Malevelent, ed., *After the Reformation: Esays in Honor of J. H. Hexter*, 247–65. Philadelphia: University of Pennsylvania Press, 1980.

Miller, James. *The Passion of Michel Foucault*. New York: Doubleday, 1993.

Miller, Perry. *The New England Mind: From Colony to Province*. Boston: Beacon, 1953.

Mitford, Nancy. *The Pursuit of Love*. New York: Random House, 1946.

Morgan, Edmund. *Visible Saints: The Story of a Puritan Idea*. New York: New York University Press, 1963.

Morson, Gary Saul. "For the Time Being: Sideshadowing, Criticism, and the Russian Countertradition." In Nancy Easterlin and Barbara Riebling, eds., *After Poststructuralism*, 203–31. Evanston: Northwestern University Press, 1993.

Murdoch, Iris. "The Sublime and the Beautiful Revisited." *Yale Review* 40, no. 2 (1959): 247–71.

——. *The Sovereignty of Good*. New York: Schocken, 1971.

Newfield, Christopher, and Ronald Strickland, eds. *After Political Correctness*. Boulder: Westview, 1995.

Nicholson, Linda, ed. *Feminism/Postmodernism*. New York: Routledge, 1990.

Nozick, Robert. *The Examined Life*. New York: Simon and Schuster, 1989.

Nussbaum, Martha. *Love's Knowledge*. New York: Oxford University Press, 1990.

Ohmann, Richard. "English after the USSR." In Christopher Newfield and Ronald Strickland, *After Political Correctness*, 226–37. Boulder: Westview, 1995.

Palmer, Frank. *Literature and Moral Understanding*. Oxford: Clarendon, 1992.

Parker, David. "Evaluative Discourse and the Return of the Repressed." *The Critical Review* 31 (1991), 3–14.

——. *Ethics, Theory, and the Novel*. Cambridge: Cambridge University Press, 1994.

Pipes, Richard. *The Russian Revolution*. New York: Vintage, 1991.

——. *Russia under the Bolshevik Regime*. New York: Vintage, 1995.

Plath, Sylvia. *Ariel*. New York: Harper and Row, 1965.

Porte, Joel. *The Romance in America*. Middleton: Wesleyan University Press, 1969.

Porter, Roy. *Mind-Forg'd Manacles*. Cambridge, Mass.: Harvard University Press, 1987.

Prendergast, Christopher. *The Order of Mimesis*. Cambridge: Cambridge University Press, 1986.

Price, Martin. *Forms of Life*. New Haven: Yale University Press, 1983.

Putnam, Hilary. *Realism with a Human Face*. Cambridge, Mass.: Harvard University Press, 1990.

Riebling, Barbara. "Remodeling Truth, Power, and Society: Implications of Chaos Theory, Nonequilibrium Dynamics, and Systems Science for the Study of

Politics and Literature." In Nancy Easterlin and Barbara Riebling, eds., *After Poststructuralism*, 177–201. Evanston: Northwestern University Press, 1993.

Robinson, Harlow. "The Death of Russian Beauty." *New York Times Book Review*, January 19, 1994, 14.

Rothenberg, Paula. "Form versus Substance in Socialist Democracy." In Stephen Rosskamm Shalom, ed., *Socialist Visions*, 45–50. Boston: South End Press, 1983.

Said, Edward. "Opponents, Audiences, Constituencies, and Communities." *Critical Inquiry* 9, no. 1 (1982): 1–26.

———. "The Politics of Knowledge." In Paul Berman, ed., *Debating P. C.*, 172–89. New York: Dell, 1992.

———. "Fantasy's Role in the Making of Nations." Review of Jacqueline Rose, *States of Fantasy*. *TLS*, August 9, 1996, 7–8.

Saldivar, Ramon. *Chicano Narrative: The Dialectics of Difference*. Madison: University of Wisconsin Press, 1990.

Scheick, William. "New England Puritanism and the New Left." *Thought Quarterly Review* 49 (1971): 72–82.

Searle, John. "Reiterating the Differences: A Reply to Derrida." *Glyph* 1 (1977): 198–208.

———. "Literary Theory and Its Discontents." In Dwight Eddins, ed., *The Emperor Redressed*, 166–98. Tuscaloosa: University of Alabama Press, 1995.

Seaton, James. *Cultural Conservatism, Political Liberalism*. Ann Arbor: University of Michigan Press, 1996.

Shi, David. *Facing Facts*. New York: Oxford University Press, 1995.

Shklar, Judith. *The Face of Injustice*. New Haven: Yale University Press, 1990.

Snitow, Ann, Christine Tansell, and Sharon Thompson, eds. *Powers of Desire*. New York: Monthly Review Press, 1983.

Spielmann, Peter James. "Aborigine Award Provides Another Hoax in Australia." *Austin American Statesman*, March 14, 1997, 11.

Spivak, Gayatri Chakravorty. "The New Historicism: Political Commitment and the Postmodern Critic." In H. Aram Veeser, ed., *The New Historicism*, 277–92. London: Routledge, 1989.

Stivers, Richard. *The Culture of Cynicism*. Oxford: Blackwell, 1994.

Stone, Lawrence. "Madness." *New York Review of Books*, December 16, 1982, 28–36.

———. "Lawrence Stone Replies." *New York Review of Books*, March 31, 1982, 42–44.

Szymborska, Wislawa. *View with a Grain of Sand*. Translated by Stanislaw Baranczak and Clare Cavanagh. San Diego: Harcourt Brace, 1995.

Tan, Amy. "In the Canon for All the Wrong Reasons." *Harper's Magazine* 293 (1996): 27–31.

Terdiman, Richard. "The Politics of Political Correctness." In Christopher Newfield and Ronald Strickland, eds., *After Political Correctness*, 238–52. Boulder: Westview, 1995.

Tuttleton, James W. *The Novel of Manners in America*. Chapel Hill: University of North Carolina Press, 1972.

Tuveson, Ernest Lee. *Redeemer Nation*. Chicago: University of Chicago Press, 1968.

Vance, Carole S., ed. *Pleasure and Danger*. Boston: Routledge and Kegan Paul, 1984.

Veeser, Harold Aram, ed. *The New Historicism*. London: Routledge, 1989.

Walker, Clarence E. *Deromanticizing Black Literary History*. Knoxville: University of Tennessee Press, 1991.

Walker, Ralph W. S. "What He Really Means." *TLS*, January 3, 1997, 10.

Warhol, Robyn R., and Diane Price Herndl, eds. *Feminisms*. New Brunswick, N.J.: Rutgers University Press, 1991.

Watson, George. *The Certainty of Literature*. New York: Harvester, 1989.

Watts, Steven. "The Idiocy of American Studies: Poststructuralism, Language, and Politics in the Age of Self-Fulfillment." *American Quarterly* 43, no. 4 (1991): 625–60.

Weinauer, Emily. "Plagiarism and the Proprietary Self: Policing the Boundaries of Authorship in Herman Melville's 'Hawthorne and His Mosses.'" *American Literature* 69, no. 4 (December 1997): 697–717.

Wharton, Edith. *Summer*. New York: Harper and Row, 1980.

Whitebook, Joel. "The Politics of Redemption." *Telos* 63 (1985): 156–68.

Williams, Raymond. *Keywords*. Oxford: Oxford University Press, 1976.

Wilson, William Julius. *When Work Disappears*. New York: Knopf, 1996.

Wimsatt, William Kurtz, Jr., and Monroe Beardsley. "The Intentional Fallacy." In William Kurtz Wimsatt, Jr., *The Verbal Icon*. New York: Farrar, Straus, and Cudahy, 1960: 3–18.

Wood, Gordon. *The Radicalism of the American Revolution*. New York, Vintage, 1993.

Young, Iris Marion. "The Ideal of Community and the Politics of Difference." In Linda Nicholson, ed., *Feminism/Postmodernism*, 300–27. New York: Routledge, 1990.

Index